WOMANBEING
AND
WOMANSELF

WOMANBEING
AND
WOMANSELF

Characters in Black Women's Novels

PHANUEL AKUBUEZE EGEJURU

iUniverse, Inc.
Bloomington

Womanbeing and Womanself:
Characters in Black Women's Novels

iUniverse books may be ordered through booksellers or by contacting:

iUniverse
1663 Liberty Drive
Bloomington, IN 47403
www.iuniverse.com
1-800-Authors (1-800-288-4677)

Because of the dynamic nature of the Internet, any Web addresses or links contained in this book may have changed since publication and may no longer be valid. The views expressed in this work are solely those of the author and do not necessarily reflect the views of the publisher, and the publisher hereby disclaims any responsibility for them.

Any people depicted in stock imagery provided by Thinkstock are models, and such images are being used for illustrative purposes only.

Certain stock imagery © Thinkstock.

ISBN: 978-1-4502-6520-1 (sc)
ISBN: 978-1-4502-6521-8 (ebk)

Printed in the United States of America

iUniverse rev. date: 6/25/2011

DEDICATION

TO MY SISTER MARY:
THE EPITOME OF WOMANSELF

TABLE OF CONTENTS

WOMANBEING AND WOMANSELF

Quite often, we have this feeling of déjà vu, of the familiar, and we start groping for words to describe it or for faces to pin on it. At other times, we run into someone or a group of people who have experienced something that we too have experienced. We all start talking about this familiar "phenomenon" to which we assign different names, names that do not exactly capture the totality of our combined experiences. Now, think of this phenomenon as the sum total of all the negative treatments and conditions directed specifically at women in societies across the globe. In Victorian England for instance, thinkers, politicians and writers referred to this phenomenon as The Woman Question. In the twentieth century, it became Women's Issues. But these labels are still too broad based to encapsulate that indescribable state of being that majority of the world's women go through all their lives or part of their lives. It is this sense of the familiar, this déjà vu yet singularly un-named manner of existence peculiar to women that is identified in this book as Womanbeing.

Being, the present participle of the verb to be is generally understood to refer to some entity that exists or something that is. As a human entity and like other entities, animate or inanimate, woman exists; she has a state of being. In this state, a woman's being approximates the being explored by Jean Paul Sartre in his classic theory of *Being and Nothingness*. For Sartre, there are two components to Being. There is *Being-in-itself* (en-soi), a state that is "fixed, complete, wholly given, absolutely contingent, with no reason for its being; it is roughly the equivalent to the inert world of objects and things." This Being-in-itself hides within its confines, another entity called *Being-for-itself* (pour-soi), a state that is incomplete, fluid, indeterminate; it corresponds to the being of human consciousness (Magill, p.2271). Sartre's two categories of being are closely related to woman's being and self.

The dictionary meaning of being is modified when the word is prefixed with woman to create the word womanbeing. Here's a tentative explanation of the genesis of Womanbeing. Like so many ills that confront woman, her original being has been modified because of her association with man. As far as we know, there is no documentary evidence showing how and at what stage in human evolution, man became the ruler and the giver of laws in human society. All we have are myths and folktales (including the bible creation story in Genesis) telling us how man and woman were created. We learned how they reproduced, multiplied their kind and formed communities or societies. There are also a number of "Why Stories" from various African communities that explain why men became the dominant partners and rulers over their womenfolk. Myths and folktales served well for humans in their hunting and gathering stages. Indeed, they continued to serve as reference points for "civilized" societies. However, humans have progressed well beyond the primitive stage and do not need myths and folktales to figure out how man arrived at his present stage of dominance and ruler-ship. One would hazard to conjecture that it is thanks to man's superior physical strength and brutal force that he was able to claim and solidify his dominance and governance in society. Having secured his position of power, he then proceeded to assign roles and positions to male and female members of his society. It was perhaps at this juncture that man started to impose himself and his will on woman. In turn, woman lost the autonomy of her primordial being along with the ability to define and assert her action-based unique self. Ultimately human being became synonymous with man, an entity or a word that supposedly subsumed woman. Having swallowed woman so to speak, man spat (vomited) her out in a new form—womanbeing.

Simply defined, Womanbeing is a state of being and living as prescribed and imposed on woman by man and society. This society and man presumed that woman is weak and must of necessity depend upon man for support physically, mentally, emotionally, psychologically and economically. Because of her supposed fragile nature, society assigns to woman, tasks that are purportedly easy on her physical and mental states. Therefore, woman's duties include childbearing, child rearing and house keeping with all its ramifications. She is thus trapped in a specific mold in terms of self-fulfilling jobs that are traditionally reserved for man. Under pretext of protecting woman, the men in her life, father, husband or lover exploit her and inflict all kinds of abuses on her. To compound her problems, society discourages woman from questioning the role, the status and the treatment she receives from society. If she dared to question, she was viewed as deranged or misguided, and for her own good, must be locked up in the home or sent to a mental institution for management. For her physical survival therefore, woman meekly accepted the role and place assigned to her by society. With relentless brainwashing meant to secure her firmly in the slot created for her, she eventually succumbed to societal pressure to "remain in her place."

In *Key Ideas in Human Thought*, self is defined as "an aware subject, the subject of mental ability, the thing that thinks, feels and wills. Above all, it is the subject as he or she experiences himself or herself (McLeish, 668)" Various definitions of self appear in many dictionaries. One dictionary defines self as an individual's consciousness of his own being or identity; ego.

The self in Womanself involves more than the dictionary and encyclopedia definitions because they are too general. Woman's self in the context of this study is closer to Sartre's *Being-for-itself* which "lies coiled in the heart of being like a worm." In the same way, woman's self lies dormant inside Womanbeing. Although Womanbeing is created, exploited and ruled by society, there comes a time when the self within the being rebels and emerges to reclaim its own separate identity from being. Thus, Womanself could be defined as a state of freedom arising out of liberation from the shackles of Womanbeing. In other words, Womanself emerges in reaction to societal rules and impositions on Womanbeing. As G.H. Mead phrased it, "To understand a self means to understand something about the roles and attitudes of others as product of that self. Without society involving a number of different roles, there would be nothing in terms of which a self could arise (Magill, 2083)." The difference between man's self and woman's self lies in the treatment that each receives from society. Whereas society expects and encourages man's self to emerge and flourish, society does everything in its power, not only to discourage the emergence of woman's self, it also tries to smother and destroy woman's self if it emerged.

A distinctive feature of womanself is the ability to choose and act upon its choices. Because society is used to womanbeing that should not and does not choose, it inaccurately sees womanself as rebellious. As dramatized by female characters in black women's novels, womanself is neither rebellious nor anti-society. It recognizes and approves of complimentary roles of men and women for the survival and welfare of the human society. Indeed, this idea of complimentary roles for both genders is eloquently articulated by Mariama Ba in the closing chapter of her *So Long A Letter*:

I remain persuaded of the inevitable and necessary complimentarity of man and woman . . . Love, imperfect as it may be in its content and expression, remains the natural link between these two beings . . . The success of the family is born of a couple's harmony, as the harmony of multiple instruments creates a pleasant symphony. However, womanself insists on women making their own choices, living as themselves and for themselves, not for the men in their lives.

It is not surprising that black women writers, especially the novelists, consistently focus on their fellow black women as subject of their novels. The reason for this should be clear to serious scholars and other readers of black literature. Black men novelists showed little interest in representing women, and when they did, they relegated women characters to the margin. Women in black men's novels never made it to the center stage just as they never took center stage in real life. That women were not regularly represented in men's novels is not to say that men purposely excluded them out of malice or spite. Men, the world over, were just being true to their worlds and their cultures. In their worlds, women did not matter; when it was necessary to include women, the men spoke for and about their women. And since the world of fiction reflects the world of reality and since a mind-set is a terrible enemy to fight, one should not be in haste to condemn men's novels as anti-women. It would be left to women to speak for and about themselves. This explains why black women novelists automatically took on the role of spokeswomen for the general population of black women.

Even in this twenty-first century, the attitude of black men towards black women has not changed much from what it used to be centuries back. And it must be emphasized that black men's attitude towards black women is shaped by a culture that grossly undervalues women to the point of reification. Of course, this objectification of women is not peculiar to men of African descent. Men of European and Asian descents also reified their women for centuries. It is a well-known fact that women in India are still reified and so grossly undervalued that pregnant women in India now routinely use ultrasound as an instrument for screening off unwanted female fetuses.

Indeed, some of the names given to female children in parts of black Africa speak volumes to the value or the lack thereof assigned to women in African societies. For instance, among the Igbo of Nigeria, most names given to baby girls insinuate that girls are merely tolerated and serve only as "half-bread." In the early 1960's, a baby girl born in my kindred was named Ria Ria ka njo, shortened to Ria Ria. Literally Ria Ria means "Nothing" and ka njo means "worse than." This baby's name is a statement claiming: "Having no children at all is worse than having only girls." This name is considered most appropriate given the circumstances of this baby's birth. You see, Ria Ria's mother who was the first wife of her husband, had four girls before Ria Ria. Thus, the name is meant as a consolation to the couple, especially to the wife, because, the husband can always marry other wives to bear male children for him. In fact, Ria Ria's father had already taken other wives after Ria Ria's mother had two girls in a row. In this name therefore, we see how a girl is placed next to "Nothing". Actually, Ria Ria as a name, ranks lower than Nwanyibuife-Woman is something—another name that seemingly confers a positive value on a girl even though this name virtually has an identical meaning as Ria Ria ka njo. Both names are meant to console parents who desperately hoped for a boy only to get yet another girl! In the same time period, a baby boy in the same kindred was named Ke wu nwa which literally means "The Real Child." One can only imagine how a girl with a name like RiaRia ka njo would feel when she grows up and realizes that she is only a "half-for-do." One can also imagine how she would feel when she realizes that the choice for her parents was between her and "Nothing." As for Ke wu nwa, there is no need to ask how he would feel knowing that he is "The Real Child" whose coming his parents had been praying and hoping for.

Here then is a culture that lets a girl know right from birth that she is next to "Nothing" while a boy is "Everything." Through its naming system, this society demonstrates how it fosters a feeling of inferiority among its women and a feeling of superiority among its men. This society makes it plain to women that they have no choice but to accept and endure the fact that they are not appreciated but tolerated. It is in cultures such as this that the condition of womanbeing is drummed into the psyche of very young girls like Nnu Ego's twin girls in Emecheta's *The Joys of Motherhood* and Tambudzai and her sisters in Dangarembga's *Nervous Conditions*. At the age when children are in kindergarten or first grade, Nnu Eo's twins, Kehinde and Taiwo must go to the waterside to fetch firewood that their mother retails. They must take charge of fetching water to water the vegetable garden. And when Taiwo suggested that "the boys can help too", their mother reminded her: "They have to go to their lesson, Taiwo; and stop moaning. You are a girl, you know." "I know that mother. You remind us all the time." Later Taiwo grumbled: "The boys have the evening off for their stupid lessons, and they're let off from going to fetch the wood that we have to sell to feed us." Nnu Ego who couldn't take Taiwo's complaints any longer shouted: "But you are girls! They are boys. You have to sell to put them in a good position in life, so they will be able to look after the family. When your husbands are nasty to you, they will defend you." It is already assumed that the girls will marry. It is also assumed that their husbands will be nasty to them! It is by hearing adults constantly reminding girls that they are inferior to boys that boys develop their superiority complex and their inflated sense of self. Thus, when Adaku, Nnu Ego's co-wife tells Nnu Ego's son, Oshia to go along with her daughter Dumbi to fetch water, the boy yelled: "I'm not going! I am a boy. Why should I help in the cooking? That's a woman's job." In the same vein, Tambudzai resented the fact that she and her sister Netsai had to leave other chores to go and fetch their brother Nhamo's luggage from the bus station. Tambudzai says: "Knowing that he did not help, that he only wanted to demonstrate to us and to himself that he had the power, the authority to make us do things for him, I hated fetching my brother's luggage. When she was told that she had to stop school because there was just enough money for her brother's fees, Tambu was devastated and she sought her brother's sympathy. What we hear instead is the following conversation:

"Don't you know I am the one who has to go to school?"

"But I want to go to school."

"Wanting won't help."

"Why not?"

"It's the same everywhere. Because you are a girl. That's what Baba said remember?"

Tambu's father rubs it in further by taunting her: "Can you cook books and feed them to your husband? Stay at home with your mother. Learn to cook and clean. Grow vegetables."

To add to Tambudzai's consternation, her mother supports her father. She reminds her daughter that, "even Maiguru knew how to cook and clean and grow vegetables. She adds in a tone of consolation to her daughter:

This business of womanhood is a heavy burden. How could it not be? Aren't we the ones who bear the children? When it is like that you just can't decide today I want to do this, tomorrow I want to do that, the next day I want to be educated! When there are sacrifices to be made, you are the one who has to make them. As these things are not easy, you have to start learning them early, from a very early age. The earlier the better so that it is easy later on . . . What will help you, my child, is to learn to carry your burdens with strength.

It is because of this type of conditioning that Owerri women in Nigeria still announce and "celebrate" the birth of every newborn with the following song:

9

Onye di ime? O wu anyi. Onye k' ime n'eme? O wu anyi.
Onye n'ebe akwa?

O wu anyi. Onye nyiri kpuu? O wu anyi. Onye muru nwa?
O wu anyi.

Onye sachara nwa? O wu anyi. Onye hichara nshi? O wu anyi.
Onye chiri ara?

O wu anyi. Ahuhu di n'omumu? Nke anyi. Onu di n'omumu?
Nke anyi.

Umu nwanyi ibe m . . . le-le-le. Unu gbakota . . . le-le-le. K'anyi
ruma uwa . . . le-le-le.

Who is pregnant? We are. Who is in labor? We are. Who is
crying? We are.

Who is pushing? We are. Who is delivered? We are. Who is
bathing baby?

We are. Who is wiping baby's shit? We are. Who is nursing
baby? We are.

Trepidations of birthing belong to us. The joys of birthing
belong to us.

My fellow women . . . le-le. Let's come together . . . le-le. And
endure our fate . . . le-le.

Strange as it may sound, this song of lamentation is
"celebratory" for these women; they sing and dance to it with
vigor and abandon. So, one doubts that women with this type
of mind-set would question, let alone try to rise above their
state of womanbeing. What are the chances that boys who
grew up watching adults "put girls in their place" would be
nice and respectful towards their future wives or lovers?

Until black women writers came along to reveal the hidden
world and untold stories of black women, no one thought of

questioning the stories that men told of their world and their people. Whatever they wrote was considered "representative" of their communities. It is most interesting to note that a few black women novelists-Flora Nwapa, Maraima Ba and Toni Morrison paid homage to China Achebe, who they claimed, inspired them to write after reading his *Things Fall Apart*. One wonders what these novelists found so irresistible in Achebe's novel that compelled them to write. It is possible that what these women encountered in Achebe's novel, forced them to write stories that seemed to challenge the authenticity of men's perspectives in their representations of black communities. It appears that after reading men's novels, these women novelists like Janie in Zora Neale Hurston's *Their Eyes Were Watching God*, asked "Where is me?" But unlike Janie whose little dark self was in the picture and was pointed out to her, these women novelists didn't even find a dot that represented them in the picture of their people painted by men novelists. Therefore, in response to the blank space in the picture, women novelists undertook to insert their image in that picture. They began to write themselves into the story of their people.

For their point of departure, women novelists picked up Womanbeing, a creation of man's. As already mentioned, this creature has no life of her own; she lives for man. Novels by black women are filled with a host of womanbeings. Only a couple of female characters in women's novels did not experience the state of womanbeing. The few characters who avoided that state started from childhood to assert their womenselves. Some like Selina and Silla in Marshall's *Brown Girl, Brownstones* held on to their "selves" throughout their lives. Several characters lived the greater part of their lives in a state of womanbeing before their transition into womanself.

And there were some who repressed or completely lost the "selves' they had asserted earlier in their lives. A number of characters never made the transition from being to self, and some vacillated between the two states.

Celie: Archetypical Womanbeing:

In Alice Walker's Pulitzer Prize Winning novel-*The Color Purple*, we encounter Celie, who represents the archetypical womanbeing because she experienced every conceivable abuse that most Africa-American women endured during slavery and reconstruction years. Though Celie and her mother lived after slavery, they were virtual slaves to the men in their lives. Celie's mother died in her state of womanbeing and Celie did not break completely from being to self.

At fourteen years old, shortly before her mother's death, Celie is forced into the role of mother to her younger siblings and to the role of sexual partner to her stepfather. Totally confused, Celie could not discuss her situation with anybody in her family. She finally decided to confide in God through her unanswered letters to God. In her first letter with which the novel opens, we read the horrifying details of abuse that would last through the greater portion of her life. She writes:

Dear God,

I am fourteen years old. I have always been a good girl. Maybe you can give me a sign letting me know what is happening to me. Last spring when little Lucious come I heard them fussing. He was pulling on her arm. She say It too soon, Fonso, I ain't well. Finally he leave her alone. A week go by, he pulling on her arm again. She say Naw, I ain't gonna. Can't you see I' m already half dead, an all of these children.

Soon after the above incident, Celie's mother goes to see a doctor. She leaves Celie to take over the house chores and childcare. She unwittingly leaves Celie to take on the role of sexual partner to her stepfather who had never said a kind word to her. When he started his sexual advances to her, a confused Celie turned inquisitive eyes on him. His response to her is one sentence in her first letter to God:

"Just say you gonna do what your mammy wouldn't."

First he put his thing up gainst my hip and sort of wiggle it around. Then he grab hold my titties. Then he push his thing inside my pussy. When that hurt, I cry. He start to choke me, saying You better shut up and git used to it. But I don't never git used to it. And now I feels sick every time I be the one to cook. My mammy she fuss at me an look at me. She happy, cause he good to her now. But too sick to last long.

Before her mother died, Celie had become pregnant from the rapes. In her second letter she talks to God about her burden of keeping house and caring for her siblings. She talks of the painful experience of first pregnancy and the strange feeling of having a baby come out of her: *Then that little baby come out of my pussy chewing on it fist you could have knock me over with a feather.* When her mother asked who the father was, Celie said it was God's. She didn't know what else to tell her mother. In the same letter, Celie is in a hospital where she just had her second baby, a boy. She is afraid her stepfather would take this baby and kill it as he did the first one. She presumed that he took her first baby while she slept and killed it in the woods. It turned out that the baby girl was also given or sold to a childless couple. He did take the second baby and sold it to a man and his wife in Monticello. Celie is left to suffer the aching pains of her breasts filled with milk but no baby to nurse.

At last, Celie gets a break from the man's rape when he got married to a girl of Celie's age. However, the house chores and childcare got heavier for her because she is the only servant for the entire household. The man beats her for the slightest excuse such as winking at a boy in church (though she did not). When she noticed that her stepfather was developing sexual interest in her younger sister Nettie, she vowed to protect her. She advised her sister to marry an old widower known simply as Mr. In that way she figured that Nettie could have one good year out of her life before the pregnancies commenced. At the end of her fifth letter we learn that Celie is suffering from premature menopause. This condition could have been triggered by sustained trauma arising from relentless raping of the young Celie by her stepfather. Talking about pregnancy she says: "But me, never again. A girl at church say you git big if you bleed every month. I don't bleed no more."

Celie's dream of marriage for her sister would not materialize because their stepfather would not allow Nettie to marry Mr. He claimed he had better and bigger plans for Nettie. He would like her to get an education and become a school teacher. Fortunately, Nettie ran away for good and thus avoided the fate of her sister. The step father told Mr. that he would be happy to trade Celie for Nettie. He proceeded to point out to Mr. the bad and the good sides of marrying Celie instead of Nettie:

She ain't fresh. She spoiled. Twice. But you don't need a fresh woman no how. She ugly. But she no stranger to hard work. And she clean. And God fixed her. You can do everything just like you want to and she ain't gonna make you feed it or clothe it. Fact is, I got to get rid of her . . . She too old to be living at home. She'd come with her own linen. She can take that cow she raise down there back of the crib. But Nettie you flat out can't have. Not now. Not never.

Finally Mr. speaks up and says; I ain't never really looked at that one. The step father continues to haggle and says:

Well, next time you come you can look at her. She ugly. Don't even look like she kin to Nettie. But she'll make the better wife. She aint's smart either. But she can work like a man. And another thing-She tell lies.

Mr. goes away without making up his mind. When the woman working for him quits, Mr. goes back to have a second look at Celie. At this time, she is subjected to the treatment of a slave on the auction block. After listening to further advantages of having Celie, Mr. accepts her along with her cow.

Here then is a perfect picture of a womanbeing, completely dehumanized and traded away like an unwanted burdensome piece of furniture. Celie's unbelievable nightmarish life started on what could pass for her wedding day. She spent it running away from her husband's twelve-year old son "who picked up a rock and laid my head open. The blood run all down tween my breasts. His daddy say Don't do that! But that's all he say." After she cleaned and put a bandage on the wound, she cooked dinner, washed and combed the girls' hair as they cried and screamed themselves to sleep. In bed she couldn't sleep: "I lay there thinking bout Nettie while he on top of me."

Throughout her life with Mr. Celie served as a housekeeper, a field hand, a work horse, a sex partner and a punching bag for her husband. In addition to the burden of physical labor, Celie had to endure constant verbal abuse and vilification from Mr. Sex with Mr. was a routine job that she hated so much. She got some reprieve from her husband's verbal and physical abuses when Shug Avery, her husband's former lover, returned from her wanderings seriously ill. Celie who had heard heartwarming stories about Shug, had fallen in love with a photograph of Shug. She was completely star-stricken. Although Shug was rude and nasty to Celie upon her arrival, Celie loved her so much that she paid no attention to Shug's nastiness. In fact, she felt privileged to serve her. Thus, Celie ministered to Shug and nursed her back to health in the home she shared with her husband.

When Celie asked Shug if she liked sleeping with Mr. (which she did brazenly) she replied:

"Yeah, I have to confess, I just love it. Don't you?"

"Naw, Mr—can tell you. I don't like it at all. What is it like? He git up on you, heist your nightgown round your waist, plung in. Most times I pretend I ain't there. He never know the difference. Never ast me how I feel, nothing. Just do his business. Git off, go to sleep."

It didn't take long for Shug to develop warm feelings and affection for Celie. She used her tremendous influence over Mr. to get him to stop his cruel treatment of Celie.

It was Shug, a free spirited womanself, who revealed certain things about sex that roused Celie's curiosity. Shug would become Celie's mentor and lover and would eventually remove her physically from Mr. and whisk her off to her own home in Memphis. Celie was very content to live with Shug and serve her.

Shug taught her to make pants; she provided everything Celie needed for her sewing which eventually turned into a sizeable business. In addition, Celie and her sister unexpectedly became heirs to a house and land they thought belonged to their cruel stepfather but actually belonged to their biological father whom they never knew. At this point of obvious prosperity, one would expect Celie to let go of Shug's apron strings and assert and reclaim her own self. But Celie would not give serious thoughts to standing on her own and making her own choices and decisions. She is so worshipful of Shug that she is content to live with her and keep house for Shug and her new husband Grady. She is heart broken when Shug falls in love and runs off with a nineteen year-old boy, a dropout from high school. Throughout the months that Shug was away with the boy, Celie mourned and agonized. She was overjoyed when Shug got tired of the boy and sent him to finish school and returned to Celie. As long as Celie formed part of Shug's life, she didn't mind sharing Shug with other people. She finally got her wish when she convinced Shug to come and live in her big estate with her. She continued to hang on to Shug and to serve her like a faithful dog.

The most important outcome of the relationship between Celie and Shug is that Celie started to show signs of an awakening self. She developed enough guts to stand before Mr. and tell him off and curse him out. For instance, one day Celie asked Mr. if any more mail came from Nettie to her. Mr. said he wouldn't give them to her if they came. Then the following exchange took place:

"I curse you," Celie said.

"What that mean?" He asked.

"I say, until you do right by me, everything you touch will crumble."

"Who you think you is? You can't curse nobody. Look at you. You black, you pore, you ugly, you a woman. Goddam, you nothing at all."

"Until you do right by me everything you even dream about will fail."

"Whoever heard of such a thing? I probably didn't whup you ass enough."

"Every lick you hit me you will suffer twice."

"Shit, I should have lock you up. Just let you out to work."

"The jail you plan for me is the one in which you will rot."

During this exchange, Celie seemed to have been in a daze. While she was reporting the incident to Nettie she bragged about her newfound courage:

I give it to him straight, just like it come to me. And it seem to come from the trees. Then I say, You better stop talking because all I'm telling you ain't coming just from me. Look like when I open my mouth the air rush in and shape words. Then I feel Shug shake me. Celie, she say. And I come to myself. I'm pore, I'm black, I may be ugly and can't cook, a voice say to everything listening. But I'm here. Amen, say Shug. Amen, amen.

With that verbal confrontation, Celie seemed to have clipped Mr.'s wings. For instance, a few days later in Sofia's house, Mr. walked up to Celie and asked,

"How are you Celie?"

"Fine. I look in his eyes and I see he feeling scared of me. Well, good. Let him feel what I felt."

The new Celie caused Mr. to reflect on his inhumane treatment of Celie. He admitted to Celie that he had been stupid not to appreciate her when he had the chance.

"I was just too big a fool to let myself care," he said to her. Now he would like to make it up to her by reviving their relationship as husband and wife. He starts this conversation:

"We still man and wife, you know."

"Naw, we never was"

"You know, you look real good since you been up in Memphis."

"Yeah, Shug take good care of me."

"Celie, tell me the truth. You don't like me cause I'm a man?"

"Take off they pants, and men look like frogs to me. No matter how you kiss 'em, as far as I'm concern, frogs is what they stay."

"I see."

Despite this demonstration of nascent womanself, Celie felt insecure and quite unsure of her new self. She felt too intimidated to break away from Shug. She would not make her own choices though she would act on choices made for her by Shug. She felt obligated to play a subservient role to Shug. After all, she owed her freedom from Mr. to Shug. She owed her quasi-independence to Shug. Most importantly, it was Shug who found and rescued Nettie's letters to Celie, from where Mr. had hidden them for years. Prior to that discovery, Celie had lost hope of ever hearing from or seeing her sister again. Those letters helped her reconnect with Nettie and her long lost children, and she lived for the day of their eventual reunion. Celie experienced absolute happiness when her sister and her husband along with Celie's daughter and son, all returned safely from their missionary journey to Africa.

The only decision Celie ever made on her own was when she turned down the offer from Mr. to renew their defunct relationship as husband and wife. She suggested that they remain friends.

It is unlikely that Celie would have become a full fledged womanself by the end of her life. This is because the psychological damage done to her person during long years spent as a womanbeing, was much too intense to be healed. Her kind of psychic damage would need professional counseling for the rest of her life maybe. From childhood to adulthood she existed as a slave both in her parents' home and in her husband's home. She received no love or kindness from the people around her. All she knew were abuses and denigration. She came to believe that she deserved to be treated the way she had known all her life. Because she was continuously put down, called ugly, black, woman and nothing, Celie developed an incurable low self esteem. When in the end Shug came along and released her from enslavement by Mr. she could not believe she was really a free person; that she could stand on her own and make her own decisions and choices. What's more, as long as Shug stood as a central pillar in her life, Celie's womanself would remain coiled up inside her womanbeing.

WOMANBEING AND WIFEHOOD

There is an Igbo saying: Nma Nwanyi wu di—Beauty of a woman is a husband—implying that an unmarried woman is an ugly woman. Another saying goes: Nwoke a joo njo-A man is never ugly.

So, what should a woman do to become beautiful and acceptable to her society? She must strive to get married and have children. She wouldn't have any problem choosing a husband because no man is ugly in her society. As nature would have it however, men are forever in short supply. Therefore, there is always a cutthroat competition among women to secure husbands! Perhaps it is this state of affairs that spawned the saying: "It is the ambition of every woman to get married and have children." This saying quickly became a refrain that adult men and women in Africa drum into the ears of girls from very early period of their lives. Some baby girls are even betrothed at birth. Some have their cash worth declared in names given to them at birth, such as Nnu Ego-twenty bags of cowries, Ogu Iri—two hundred bags of cowries. Some are given less demeaning names to appease the father: Aku Nna-father's wealth or Nwanyi wu Aku-woman is wealth (she would fetch bride price for the father, of course).

Getting married and having children involves a woman and a man becoming wife and husband. Yet, the saying insists that it is only the woman for whom marriage is an ambition. It ignores the truth that marriage and children are even more important to a man than to a woman in Africa. For, it is the man who carries the burden of keeping his family name alive. He can only do so by getting married and having children with his wife or wives. Of course, a man can run around and have children with as many women as he runs into, but he cannot claim any of the children by these women and none of the children will bear his name because he has not married their mothers.

In African scale of values, wifehood precedes motherhood. Yet, it is the wife who is put down and under valued while the mother is elevated to the point of worship. And, though wifehood disappeared as precondition for motherhood among Africans brought to the New World in chains, mothers remained and still remain highly valued by people of African descent, in the United States and the Caribbean. Wife and Mother are two sides of the same woman. Yet, it is Wife, a state that leads to the coveted state of motherhood that most women dread.

We heard Amaka in Nwapa's *One Is Enough*, declare: I don't want to be a wife any more, a mistress yes, with a lover . . . but not a wife. She enumerated her reasons and because of those reasons she preferred to be a mistress rather than a wife. Why would a woman choose to be a mistress in a culture that places a high premium on marriage? Probably because, a mistress most often gets the greater portion of a man's love and affection, and sometimes a good portion of his money in cash and other materials of great value. For instance, Ona in *Joys of Motherhood* was a high class mistress. She was reputed for being a coy mistress who broke the heart of the great hunter, Agbadi. She refused to marry him, though she had a daughter-Nnu Ego with him. Ona was admired and envied by Agbadi's wives because she dared to refuse Agbdi's marriage offer, yet played with him like a toy throughout their relationship. Yet, Agbadi's wives didn't realize that the spoilt mistress was as much a victim of womanbeing as they were. Ona had no choice but to obey the orders of her father who could not produce male children. But he had the option whereby tradition allowed a man to keep one of his daughters in the family to produce male children to carry on her father's name. Therefore, Ona's father had maintained that she must never marry; his daughter was never going to stoop to any man. She was free to have men, however, and if she bore a son, he would take her father's name, thereby rectifying the omission nature had made. Ona was thus a pawn pushed around the chessboard by her father and her lover. She grew to love her lover and would have preferred to become his wife if her father had given his permission. Ona's secret desire to marry is exposed in her dying wish to her lover Agbadi: "However much you love our daughter Nnu Ego, see that you allow her to have a life of her own, a husband if she wants one. Allow her to be a woman." The reader would remember how Nnu Ego the wife, lived in misery and died alone on the roadside despite the "security" of marriage and seven children.

It is a paradox of mystical proportions that wifehood, a state that supposedly confers beauty, honor and fulfillment, in the same breath condemns one to eternal damnation. As young people would put it, "why does wife get such a dirty rap?" The answer lies in Womanbeing, this man-created state that allows man to reify woman and to use her in whatever capacity that serves his best interest.

We have innumerable examples in black women's novels, of wives who were abused and crippled physically, mentally and emotionally. We have already come across Celie of *The Color Purple*, Nnu Ego, Amaka and others to be discussed later, but Zora Neale Hurston's *Their Eyes Were Watching God* provides probably the best case of womanbeing and womanself doing battle in one female's body. Who can forget the beautiful scene in which young Janie, sprawled under the blossoming pear tree, watched the mystery of reproduction in nature:

She was stretched on her back beneath the pear tree soaking in the alto chant of the visiting bees, the gold of the sun and the panting breath of the breeze when the inaudible voice of it all came to her. She saw a dust-bearing bee sink into the sanctum of a bloom; the thousand sister-galyxes arch to meet the love embrace and the ecstatic shiver of the tree from root to tiniest branch creaming in every blossom and frothing with delight. So this was a marriage! She had been summoned to behold a revelation.

Like any normal healthy youth, Janie started daydreaming and wishing for love and consummation, as she walked into her Granny's kitchen to behold yet again, flies tumbling and singing, marrying and giving in marriage. Thus filled with a rosy image of marriage, her longing exploded in words: Oh to be a pear tree—any tree in bloom! With kissing bees singing of the beginning of the world! Where were the singing bees for her?

Janie didn't have too long to wonder and wait because along came the erstwhile shiftless Johnny Taylor, now turned glorious in Janie's glazed eyes, unwittingly presenting himself as her singing bees. But the romance couldn't last because her Granny bolted upright and peered out of the window and saw Johnny Taylor lacerating her Janie with a kiss. And that was it for Janie. That was the end of her childhood. She was ripe and Granny knew that her body was screaming for a mate. Granny called her for a little chat:

"Janie, youse uh 'oman, now so——."

"Naw, Nanny, naw Ah ain't no real "oman yet."

"Yeah, Janie, youse got yo' womanhood on yuh. So Ah mout ez well tell yuh whut Ah been savin' up for uh spell. Ah wants to see you married right away."

"Me, married? Naw, Naw, Nanny, no ma'am! Whut Ah know 'bout uh husband?"

"Whut Ah seen just now is plenty for me, honey, Ah don't want no trashy nigger, no breath-and-britches, lak Johnny Taylor usin' yo' body to wipe his foots on."

Janie protested and pleaded that she didn't know anybody to marry right away. But Granny had already taken care of that. She had settled on the good old widower, Logan Killicks, with a big house and sixty acres of rich farmland filled with crops. Janie was horrified because the vision of Logan Killicks was desecrating the pear tree but Janie didn't know how to tell Nanny that. Janie started to cry and protest some more but Granny slapped her face violently and caused her to listen while she recounted the horrible fate of black women in slavery or in freedom. From all she had seen and suffered, Granny told Janie: "De nigger woman is de mule uh de world so fur as Ah can see. Ah been prayin' fuh it tuh be different wid you. Lawd, Lawd, Lawd!

Like all good parents, Granny wanted her grand daughter to have a better life than she had. More importantly, she wanted her to be legally married and acquire the title of wife. It didn't matter that Janie didn't love Mr. Killicks and would prefer a younger man. All that mattered to the old woman was the "protection" that marriage to a well-to-do old man would provide. In her world, love was not part of the marriage equation, if one were lucky, love might come into the marriage later. Though Janie wasn't comforted by any of her grandmother's explanations, she hung on to the old woman's vague assurance that love might come later. She pondered over the miracles that love could perform:

Did marriage end the cosmic loneliness of the unmated? Did marriage compel love like the sun the day? Yes, she would love Logan after they were married. She could see no way for it not to come about, but Nanny and the old folks had said it, so it must be so. Husbands and wives always loved each other, and that was what marriage meant.

Janie married Logan on a Saturday evening in her Nanny's parlor. There was everything to eat in abundance. At the end Janie accompanied Logan to his lonesome dreary house in the middle of the woods. But Janie went on inside to wait for love to begin. Still in the honeymoon phase, Logan did everything he could to make Janie happy but Janie felt no love for him or from him. She hurried back to her Granny to share her concerns. When she heard all the good things that Logan had been doing for her Janie, Granny was furious at Janie:

"Well, if he do all dat whut you come in heah wid uh face long as mah arm for?"

"Cause you told me Ah mus gointer love him, and, Ah don't. Maybe if somebody was to tell me how, Ah could do it."

"You come heah wid yo' mouf full uh foolishness on uh busy day. Heah you got uh prop tuh lean on all yo' bawn days, and big protection, and everybody got tuh tip dey hat tuh you and call you Mis' Killicks, and you come worryin' me 'bout love."

Janie went on to list all the ugly and unflattering features of Mr. Killicks, features that rendered him reprehensible and unlovable. She began to cry: "Ah wants things sweet wid mah marriage lak when you sit under a pear tree and think Ah . . ." "'Tain't no use in you cryin' Janie," her Granny told her. "Youse young yet. No tellin' whut mout happen befo' you die. Wait awhile, baby, Yo' mind will change." Like Nnu Ego, Janie was stuck with an ugly old man. She felt betrayed. She walked out to the gate and looked towards the horizon for other solution but there was none. She knew now that marriage did not make love. Janie's first dream was dead, so she became a woman.

It is very remarkable how the author phrased this milestone in Janie's life. Janie has become a woman not in the sense of knowing a man but in the sense that she has stepped into the type of being that man wants her to be—an appendage and servant to man. And Janie's man/husband wasted no time in telling her what her role and place would be in their marriage. Since Janie took the place of his dead wife, she must take on her jobs too. Thus, Janie must not only cook and clean, she must chop the wood and tote it to the house. But Janie quickly told him that she wasn't going to cook any dinner if her didn't chop the wood and bring it in. Logan continued piling up chores that included preparing potato seeds for planting. To crown it all, he let her know that he had bought an extra mule for her to plow along side of him! Janie pretended as if she didn't hear that. With her self still in tact and impatient to stir her away from the path of womanbeing, Janie didn't waste time arguing, she started planning her escape.

While waiting for her husband to return, she looked again towards the road as if her plans for escape lay there, and sure enough her means of escape walked in to her yard; it was Joe Starks from Georgia passing through her town. She drew water for him to drink and they fell to talking. She told him she was married and was waiting for her husband who "had gone tuh buy a mule fuh me tuh plow." Joe saw his chance to sweet talk her and denounce Logan's treatment of her. Why, she has no business pulling a plow than a hog got with a holiday; she has no business cutting potato seeds either. "A pretty doll-baby lak you is made to sit on de front porch and rock and fan yo'self and eat p'taters dat other folks plant just special for you."

Joe Starks decided he needed to take a break for a week or two before proceeding on his way. They managed to meet everyday and Joe reeled off his plans to build a self-sufficient, all-black community in Florida. He had three hundred dollars in his pocket to prove his seriousness. Vulnerable Janie was intrigued. She imagined being a part of his life when he became the big ruler that he planned on becoming. Joe Starks read her mind and proposed to take her away from that awful farm. Janie didn't rush into his arms because she remembered her Granny whose words were still fresh and powerful, so she held back for the moment. First, she would probe her husband and find out his reaction when she broached the subject of leaving him. Meanwhile Joe pressed on: "Janie, if you think Ah aims to tole you off and make a dog outa you, youse wrong. Ah wants to make a wife outa you." Joe knew exactly what he meant by "make a wife out of you." He was actually saying, "You haven't seen anything yet, I am going to make a woman out of you; a woman in the sense of being a man's property.

That night, Janie debated the matter of leaving Logan. Finally she woke him up and said she wanted to speak to him "about us; you and me." "It's about time," he said. "S'posin' Ah wuz to run off and leave yuh sometime," Janie said. Logan was terrified by Janie's words. He tried to hide his fear under a scorn. He told her that he was sleepy; it was no time to speak about that. He taunted her: "'Tain't too many mens would trust yuh, knowin' yo' folks lak dey do." Janie retorted, "Ah might take and find somebody dat did trust me and leave yuh." Logan lashed back, claiming there were no more fools like him to tolerate a spoilt brat like her. The next morning Janie was fixing breakfast and Logan called her to come and help him move a pile of manure and Janie called back:

"You don't need mah help out dere, Logan. Youse in yo' place and Ah'm in mine." Logan replied:

"You ain't got no particular place. It's wherever Ah need yuh. Git uh move on yuh, and dat quick."

Janie then pelted him with very scathing remarks, so much so that Logan weakly charge at her with his shovel but stopped after a few steps. Instead, he threatened to come in there and cut Janie into pieces with his ax. In a tearful voice he cried: "Ah' m too honest and hard-workin' for anybody in yo' family, dat's de reason you don't want me! Ah guess some low-life nigger is grinnin' in yo' face and lyin' tuh yuh. God damn yo' hide." Janie couldn't listen any more. She hurried out of the gate and turned south. Joe Starks had promised to wait for her but she didn't care whether he was there or not, she needed to get out of there. After a short distance she realized she was still wearing the apron. She untied it and flung it into the bush and walked on. With that gesture she seemed to tear herself away from servitude that the apron represented for black women maids.

Joe was waiting for her with a hired rig. He helped her to the seat beside him. She noticed that with Joe on the chair, "it sat like some high ruling chair."

Janie didn't know how ominous and true her observation was. Joe meant to rule with a heavy hand. All the same, Janie resumed her vision of marriage as she witnessed it in nature, between the bee and the pear tree. From now on until death she was going to have flower dust and springtime sprinkled over everything. A bee for her bloom." They drove to Green Cove Springs and got married that night, just like Joe said, with new clothes of silk and wool.

Janie was happy and proud of Joe, the action man with commanding voice. Joe easily compelled the attention and respect of other men. In record time he rallied the men and development started in the black community. Joe was elected mayor. They built a post office and installed streetlights. Joe built a store and stocked it with all kinds of goods and grocery and everybody came to buy stuff from his store. The community and Joe started a rapid progress.

Face off, Janie wasn't just a wife, she was a trophy for Joe and he made sure to parade her as such. For every public event, Joe made sure that his wife out-dressed every other woman. Janie was instructed to carry herself as if she couldn't look no mo' better and no nobler if she wuz de queen of England. Janie looked so young beside her husband that people thought she was his daughter. Joe felt the stab and asserted his youth: "I god, Ah ain't nowhere near old enough to have no grown daughter. This here is mah wife." Joe's reaction to this remark on their age difference is a foreshadowing of the havoc that the age difference was going to wreak on their marriage.

The first public assertion of Joe's authority over his wife occurred on the day he was sworn in as mayor. After his acceptance speech, the crowd called for uh few words of encouragement from Mrs. Mayor Starks. But the crowd's applause was cut short by Joe who took the floor again and said, "Thank yuh fuh yo' compliments, but mah wife don't know nothin' 'bout no speech-makin'. Ah never married her for nothin' lak dat. She's uh woman and her place is in de home." That was the first blow in a series of humiliations and insults that Janie would be subjected to throughout her marriage to Joe. That evening Janie went home feeling cold.

Within a few weeks as mayor's wife, Janie noticed a growing distance between her and Joe and when he asked her how she liked being Mrs. Mayor. Janie said it was alright but added, "but don't yuh think it keeps us in uh kinda strain? Joe's jaw dropped!

"Strain? You mean the cookin' and waitin' on folks?"

"Naw, Jody, it jus' lokks lak it keeps us in some way we ain't natural wid one 'nother. You'se always off talikn' and fixin' things, and Ah feels lak Ah'm jus' markin' time. Hope it soon gits over."

"Over, Janie? I god, Ah ain't even started good. Ah told you inde very beginnin' dat Ah aimed tuh be uh big voice. You oughta be glad, 'cause dat makes uh big woman outa you."

We see now that Janie's hope of living a normal life is already dashed. Her need to fulfill herself through meaningful contribution to her society did not feature in Joe's plans. Rather, she was expected to be content and glad that her identity was through Joe, as the mayor's wife. For someone like Janie who appreciated being part of the crowd, the role and comportment of a mayor's wife as determined by Joe, brought to Janie only a feeling of coldness, fear and loneliness.

Gradually, the porch of Joe's store became a sort of recreational center for the men. They would gather to talk about day-to-day events of the city or to exchange pleasantries and gossip about one another's family. There was a long running talk about Matt's over worked lean mule. People indulged in the mule talk. Janie enjoyed the conversation and sometimes came up with her own good stories about the mule. But Joe forbade Janie from indulging because he didn't want her talking among trashy people. He cautioned her not to lose sight of her position as the mayor's wife: You'se Mrs. Mayor Starks, Janie. I god, Ah can't see what uh woman uh yo' 'stability would want tuh be treasurin' all dat gum-grease from folks dat don't even own de house de sleep in. Judging from what happened to Joe in the end, when Janie confronted him and insulted him back, it wouldn't have been beyond Joe to cut off Janie's tongue to prevent her from ever speaking in the first place.

Perhaps, the worst humiliation that Joe literally heaped on Janie's head was when he ordered her to keep her luxuriant hair tied up in rag whenever she worked in their store. It happened that Joe often saw male customers admiring Janie's hair and he resented that. One night he caught Walter standing behind Janie and brushing the back of his hand ever so slightly across the loose end of Janie's hair; Janie didn't even know or feel what he was doing. It was that night that Joe ordered Janie to tie up her hair around the store. She was there in the store for him to look at, not those others. This order was very irksome to Janie and she complained about it, but Joe was set on it. However, what Joe didn't tell Janie was how jealous he was at seeing other men figuratively wallowing in it (her hair) as she went about things in the store. Joe felt insecure despite his position and wealth. His ego was threatened and he wasn't sure he could hold on to Janie with so many admirers around her. Moreover, he knew that Janie had her own mind and could walk away with another man just as she did with him. So, he became paranoia with his surveillance and control of Janie's behavior and movements.

Things got worse for Janie by the day. She single handedly ran the store in addition to the post office attached to it. She developed a permanent headache from trying to fetch what each client wanted from the store shelves or from the post office. Keeping the accounts balanced and filing papers in their proper places became a mathematical dilemma. But Joe paid no attention to his wife's growing frustrations. He kept insisting that she could handle everything if she wanted; he wanted her to use her privileges.

Womanbeing was gradually pushing Janie's womanself to the side while the impact of wifehood weighed her down. Joe ordered her about like a servant and treated her like a child at every turn. He looked for the tiniest excuse to insult and humiliate her in public; he did all this to assert his authority over her. Janie talked very little because she was practically silenced by Joe's intimidating looks. She took refuge in silent rebellions over things as she was battered against the rock of empty privileges of a mayor's wife. For peace's sake Janie avoided arguments as much as possible. "Ah hates disagreement and confusion, so Ah better not talk. It makes it hard tuh git along," Janie said. But once in while, Janie would slip in some comment when everybody was doing the same. Such was the case on the occasion when Joe bought Matt's mule to free it from any further labor. The mule became a pet to the community and everyone applauded Joe for his magnanimous gesture. Janie then slipped in her sarcastic remark: Freein' dat mule makes uh mighty big man outa you. Something like George Washington and Abraham Lincoln. Abraham Lincol, he had de whole United States tuh rule so he freed de Negroes. You got uh town so you freed a mule. You have tuh have power tuh free things and dat makes you lak uh king uh something. Joe was mortified by Janie's remark but the crowd cheered and called her a born orator.

Joe's obnoxious treatment kept getting worse and Janie's retorts were coming more frequently. For instance, the day that mule died, the whole community was given a holiday and invited to drag the mule to edge of town for a carnivalesque funeral of sorts. Joe ordered Janie to stay back and mind the store. Janie protested and asked: How come Ah can't go long wid you tuh de draggin' out? Joe was genuinely speechless that she even thought of going. He was shocked that Janie would want to be seen at a dragging, where she would be pushing and shoving along side of crude, rag-clad folks. Janie asked, "You would be dere wid me, wouldn't yuh?" Yes, as a man and the mayor, he had to be there to officiate. But the mayor's wife is something different, besides she shouldn't be seen messing with commoners. "Ah' m surprised at yuh fuh askin'." When Joe returned all happy and in good humor, he was disappointed to find Janie feeling sad and sorry for herself. To him, she was just ungrateful for the efforts he had been making on her behalf. Here he was just pouring honor all over her; building a high chair for to sit in and overlook the world and she was here pouting over it! He couldn't understand how Janie could not appreciate the fact that too many women would be glad to be in her place.

Things finally came to a head when Joe extended his insults to the entire population of womankind. He constantly called women stupid, senseless and brainless. He claimed Somebody got to think for women and chillun and chickens and cows. They sho don't think none theirselves. In her quiet way, Janie would fight back with her tongue as much as she could but talking didn't help. Joe wanted her submission and she just wouldn't surrender it so easily so Joe kept fighting until he felt he had got it. The author comments:

So gradually, she pressed her teeth together and learned to hush. The spirit of the marriage left the bedroom and took to the living parlor. It was there to shake hands whenever company came to visit, but it never went back inside the bedroom again . . . The bed was no longer a daisy-field for her and Joe to play in . . . She wasn't petal-open anymore with him.

It took seven years of marriage to Joe for Janie to realize what it meant to be a married woman. She found that out one day he slapped her face in the kitchen because the dinner didn't come out quite right. He slapped her until she heard a ringing sound in her ears. As she stood there for a long time thinking about the beating when,

Something fell off the shelf inside her. Then she went inside there to see what it was. It was her image of Jody tumbled down and shattered. But looking at it she saw that it was never the flesh and blood figure of her dreams. Just something she had grabbed up to drape her dreams over . . . She had no more blossomy openings dusting pollen over her man, neither any glistening young fruit where petals used to be.

Janie's extended metaphor of fallen idol and shattered dream is one of the most beautiful passages in the novel. It constitutes the turning point in Janie's life with Joe. It was at that point that she finally let go her romantic notions about marriage and happiness. She went over her experiences so far and discovered that she had so many thoughts and emotions she had never expressed to Joe. She found things packed up and put away in parts of her heart where he could never find them. She was saving up feelings for some man she had never seen.

From that moment, Janie developed into two different selves. She had an inside and an outside now and she knew how not to mix them. Janie conditioned herself to sit back and watch her two selves operating at different levels at the same time. The first time it happened she *saw the shadow of herself going about tending the store and prostrating itself before Jody, while all the time she herself sat under a shady tree with the wind blowing through her hair and her clothes.* This experience became more frequent and Janie ceased to be surprised by it.

From this incident we notice Janie's womanbeing and womanself on a collision course, though her womanself would eventually have the upper hand. She would once more take control her life, make her decisions and follow them with concrete actions. She readjusted her approach to Joe's constant provocations and tirades. She knew when to retaliate with malicious words and when to crush him with silence. She completely de-vested herself of emotions for Joe. Every once in a while she would consider walking away from it all. But then she realized she was thirty-five and she would ask herself: To where? To what? The time she spent with Joe ought to count for something even if Joe turned out to be nothing. She had to find some meaning in the years she had wasted, if not life won't be nothin' but uh store and uh house.

At this point in time, Joe noticed signs of aging spreading fast all over his body. Instead of aging gracefully, he decided to pick on Janie who seemed to defy aging. He constantly accused her of not acting her age, of wearing the wrong clothes for age or posing like a teenager and on and on. With her re-emerged self ready to do battle, Joe chose the wrong time to hammer on the sensitive subject of aging. So, on this fateful day, Janie was too ready to "play the dozens" with Joe who scolded her for cutting a plug of tobacco the wrong way:

"I god amighty! A woman stay round uh store till she get old as Methusalem and still can't cut a little thing like a plug of tobacco! Don't stand dere rollin' yo' pop eyes at me wid yo' rump hangin' nearly to yo' knees!

Janie did something she had never done before in all the years of their marriage. With everybody watching, she walked to where Joe was and looked him straight in the eye and the word fight started:

"Stop mixin' up mah doings wid mah looks, Jody. When you git through tellin' me how tuh cut uh plug uh tobacco, then you kin tell me whether mah behind is on straight or not."

"Whut's dat you say, Janie? You must be out yo' head."

"Naw, Ah ain't outa mah head neither."

"You must be. Talkin' any such language as dat . . . You ain't no young gal to be getting' all insulted 'bout yo' looks . . . You'se uh ole woman, nearly forty."

"Naw, Ah ain't no young gal no mo' but den Ah ain't no old woman neither. Ah reckon Ah looks mah age too. But, Ah'm uh woman every inch of me and Ah know it. Dat's uh whole lot more'n you kin say . . . Talkin' 'bout me lookin' old! When you pull down yo' britches, you look lak de change uh life.

Needless to say, Joe was dumbfounded at Janie's boldness. His hurt was unimaginable. He reacted the only way he knew how-he struck Janie with all his might and drove her from the store.

With her retort, Janie morally and physically killed Joe. Because when those words sank in and Joe realized their full meaning, his vanity bled like a flood. In a few words, Janie robbed him of his manhood and destroyed his irresistible maleness that all men cherish . . . Not only did Joe lose his macho image, he got ill physically and took to his bed and never came out of it alive. So, in the end Joe realized that he had misjudged Janie all along, taking her silence as humility while she scorned him all the time. *Janie had been laughing at him and now she had cast down his empty armor before men and they had laughed, would keep laughing.*

For the remaining few months of his life, he barred Janie from entering his sick room. He refused any offers of services from her, including her offer to bring in a regular doctor to see him. He preferred the services of "root doctors" whose remedies made worse his condition. Janie forced her way into his sick room on the day he was actually drawing his last breath. Janie had enough time to tell him that he was going to die despite what the quacks told him to get his money. Most importantly, she made him listen to the "crimes" he committed against her in the name of marriage. She went on to tell him how disappointed she was with him:

You done lived wid me for twenty years and you don't half know me at all . . . you was so busy worshippin' de works of yo'hands . . . Listen Jody, you ain't de Jody ah run off down the road wid. You'se whut's left after he died. Ah run off to keep house wid yuh in uh wonderful way. But yuh wasn't satisfied wid me de way Ah was. Naw! Mah own mind had tuh be squeezed and crowded out tuh make room for your in me . . . All dis bowin'down, all dis obedience under yo'voice—dat ain't whut Ah rushed off down de road tuh find out about you.

"Git outa heah!"

Joe's last words were his orders to Janie—Get out of here! Even then Janie was full of pity for him as she looked at his dead face. "Dis sittin' in de high chair is been hard on Jody." She wondered if there was anything she could have done to help him be the man she had imagined him to be; she couldn't find anything. Before she let out the cry to let people know that Joe had expired, she went to the mirror to look at what was left of her self. The young girl was gone, but a handsome woman had taken her place. Janie's first act of liberation was to tear off the rag from her head and comb her plentiful hair; then she tied it back. *Then she starched and ironed her face, forming it into just what people wanted to see.* In other words, Janie set up the face of her womanbeing (the outside face she usually put on while the face of her womanself stayed behind) before she opened the window and cried, "Come heah people! Jody is dead. Mah husband is gone from me."

Janie maintained her double selves until after Joe's funeral because she wanted people to keep on thinking that she was the type of wife that Joe had made them believe she was. For the funeral therefore, Janie again starched and ironed her face and put on a veil. She sent her outside self to the funeral while the inside went off on a picnic: She sent her face to Joe's funeral, and herself went rollicking with the springtime across the world. Returning from the funeral, she continued to celebrate her freedom by burning all the head rags. She went about the next day with her hair in one thick braid swinging well below her waist.

Joe's death effectively meant the resurrection of Janie's complete person. From that moment she would have the rest of her life to do as she pleased. No sooner was Joe's casket lowered into the grave, than men came calling on Janie. They pelted her with their worn out clichés on woman's need for a man: "A woman by herself is a pitiful thing. The need aid and assistance. God never meant them to try to stand by themselves. Mrs. Starks, you need a man." But Janie had learned from Logan and Joe, what a husband wants from a wife-a total surrender of her body and her soul to his will. She was not in any rush to marry again and even if she wished to, it must be on her own terms.

Janie did many things to demonstrate that her self was in charge. She decided not to wear mourning clothes and mourning face longer than she personally desired. When her friend Pheoby cautioned her to mind how she seemed to be mocking Joe with her I-don't-care attitude, she told her she wasn't worried about people and their thinking. "I just love this freedom," she said. To damn them all, she threw all caution to the wind and started seeing Tea Cake, a man almost half her age, a man that people saw as a good-for-nothing bum. She intuitively knew that Tea Cake would be "right" for her. Tea Cake saw her as a person and respected her. While her former husbands only sent her about doing backbreaking chores, Tea Cake's first invitation to her was to join him in a game of chess that she knew nothing about. Somebody wanted her to play. Somebody thought it natural for her to play. He taught her to play chess, to fish and even to shoot and hunt. They fished and hunted together and they cooked and cleaned together.

Tea Cake admired her and combed her hair while she slept in his arms. Tea Cake's appreciation of her beauty was genuine just like his love was.

Like most people in love, Janie went through a period of doubt and anxiety over Tea Cake's feelings for her and she for him. She tried to compare him with other men but Tea Cake was simply different in a most positive way.

She couldn't make him look just like any other man to her. He looked like the love thoughts of women. He could be a bee to a blossom—a pear tree blossom in the spring. He seemed to be crushing scent out of the world with his footsteps. Crushing aromatic herbs with every step he took. Spices hung about him. He was a glance from God.

Tea Cake equally perceived her as a glance from God. While Janie remained skeptical he reassured her with: "Nobody else on earth kin hold uh candle tuh you, baby. You got de keys to de kingdom." When Janie realized that Tea Cake was for real she decided to go all the way. Then Tea Cake started to shower her with flattery and tender loving care. He swept her off to a community picnic, an indirect way of declaring their love publicly.

After watching Janie's carryings on with Tea Cake for a while, her friend Pheoby came over to caution her again and to let her know that she was taking an awful chance with Tea Cake. Again Janie reassured her that she knew exactly what she was doing. Besides, she's doing no more than she did when she took chances with marriage before. Now Janie "is doing her own thing." She told Pheoby that Tea Cake was dragging her to some place she didn't want to go; she had always wanted to go places but Joe didn't allow her. "Ah wants tuh utilize mahself all over, she added.

Janie chose to marry Tea Cake. She sold her store for she planned to move elsewhere with him. She brazenly announced to Pheoby: "So, us is goin' off somewhere and start all over in Tea Cake's way. Dis ain't no business proposition, and no race after property and titles. Dis is uh love game. Ah done lived Grandma's way, now Ah means tuh live mine."

Janie and Tea Cake got married by a preacher in Jacksonville and they started their love game of a marriage in earnest. Though Janie was rich in cash and property, Tea Cake told her that he would work and earn a living for both of them. So, he told her they would go to the Everglades where work was plentiful in the muck. "Folks don't do nothin' down dere but make money and fun and foolishness. We must go dere," he told Janie. When Tea Cake dozed off, Janie looked down on him and felt a self-crushing love. So her soul crawled out from its hiding place.

In the end, Janie and Tea Cake experienced the dream love and marriage that Janie had witnessed while she lay under the pear tree more than twenty years before. Tea Cake taught her the maiden language all over. They were literally inseparable. Tea Cake would rush back from the farm in the afternoon, just to spend time with Janie. It reached a point when Janie decided to go and work along side of him in the muck. At the end of the day they came home to cook and clean and eat together. Tea Cake never tired of telling her how beautiful she was and how lucky he was to be with her. Their happiness was so complete that one could bet that they would "live happily ever after," if a hurricane hadn't intervened to shorten their time together. While they were trying to float to safety Tea Cake was bitten by a rabid dog, as he tried to save Janie from the dog. In a most ironic twist of fate, Tea Cake died from a gunshot fired at him by Janie. Although Janie's act was purely in self-defense, it was equally a genuine act of euthanasia; she effectively ended Tea Cake's misery from the terrible illness. Looking closely at Tea Cake's death, one could see it as a Christ-like sacrifice for his beloved Janie. And is there greater love than this that a man gave up his life for his loved one? It was Joe's death that led to the re-emergence of Janie's womanself. But it was Tea Cake's love, encouragement and all round support for Janie that fanned her hesitant and smoldering womanself into roaring flame, causing it to flourish.

The question that most readers ask is this, why did Janie continue to stay on with Joe for twenty years when she had already discovered that their marriage was practically dead in the seventh year? She was twenty-four at that point and she could have walked away as she did before but she didn't. I believe she weighed the situation and studied her husband. She probably realized that time was on her side, and unless Joe resorted to outright murder, she would wait him out. Although Janie presented herself as a naïve adolescent when she got married to Logan and Joe, she matured as their cruelty taught her to become shrewd. Thus, she knew she was the sole heir in the event of Joe's demise. It was this realization more than anything that caused her to question the rationale for leaving, because she did consider that option at thirty-seven after a beating from Joe: Now and again she thought of a country road at sun-up and considered flight. She cautioned herself not to dismiss Joe as nothing because he definitely is something in my mouth. He's got tuh be else Ah ain't got nothin' tuh live for.

Having carefully evaluated the "battle" with Joe, she found herself pressed to the wall. Joe was determined to "break"

Janie like a trainer breaks a work animal. He would not stop till he felt he had her submission. She then devised a ruse, an ingenious survival tactic to deal with Joe. She split her person into two. The outside or her womanbeing went about bowing to Joe and doing his biddings. The outside was participating in a show to entertain an audience whose applause Joe needed to flatter and sustain his ego. Her womanself remained inside, planning and guiding her actions.

It must be pointed out that Janie was not beaten into submission. Her remaining with Joe wasn't a question of no option but a conscious choice coupled with shrewd planning to fight to the finish. She survived, thanks to her resilient self that worked with her being to save her person. Janie killed Joe with a few deadly words: "When you pull down yo' britches, you look lak de change uh life."

On the other hand, her life with Tea Cake is like a fairytale with a moral tag-a wife needs a loving and cooperative husband to achieve self actualization.

SILENCE OF DEAD-LIVING WOMEN

W e do not hear the muffled cry, the inward screaming and kicking of women who silently endure equally abusive treatment like their more vocal and combative sisters. Yet, a greater number of women suffer "silent death" from wifehood. Death in this context is not physical termination of life. It is the death of a person's true self, the taking away of someone's identity; it is the death of all desire to be one's own self. Among the women dead-but-living are Shingayi and Maiguru in Dangarembga's *Nervous Conditions*; Ruth and her two daughters, Corinthians and Magdalene in Toni Morrison's *Song of Solomon*. There are innumerable dead-but-living women but the few here help to put faces on the problem.

Tambudzai, the narrator of *Nervous Conditions* cautioned the reader: My story is not after all about death, but about my escape and Lucia's; about my mother's and Maiguru's entrapment; and about Nyasha's rebellion. The narrator's story might not be about the physical death of any of the five people but it did dwell on the victimization of them all by their own femaleness. It did explore in particular the dead-but-living situation of her aunt Maiguru and her mother Shingayi. Because these two women were wives, they silently suffered "death" of their true selves.

Before Shingayi became a permanent invalid as a result of her chronic pregnancy, she used to be active in gardening, childcare and house chores. Talking about her mother's daily routine Tambudzai said: "My mother, lips pressed tight, would hitch little Rambanai more securely on her back and continue silently at her labours." She had enough experience of womanbeing to prepare and forewarn her daughter that being a woman was a burden because you had to bear children and look after them and the husband. A wife did not only give birth to children, she was even expected to prevent them from dying! If they died she must continue to give birth to replace her dead children. Shingayi was very unlucky because she just couldn't get her children to live! She started by losing her firstborn son who died at the age of five. It was because of that first premarital pregnancy that she was forced to marry the poverty-stricken Jeremiah, the father of her baby. Then she lost three boys and one girl in a row. The only way to deal with her losses was to continue breeding more babies to replace the dead children.

Even before she lost these children, Shingayi's position at Jeremiah's family was very precarious. You see, her marriage to Jeremiah did not exactly follow the traditional protocol. At fifteen she was impregnated by Jeremiah, whose father couldn't afford her bride price. To save face, her father "tied" her to Jeremiah with little or no bride price. Because Jeremiah was not a willing groom, Shingayi had the extra burden of securing her position as a legitimate wife by producing many children. The frequent pregnancies led to maternal depletion which in turn left her very fragile, physically and emotionally. To save her from outright mortal death, it was suggested without her knowledge that her younger sister Lucia, be brought in as a second wife for Jeremiah. Lucia would ease her sister's burden with child bearing. At the same time she would help with farm work, gardening and housework. The plan was rejected by Babamukuru, the well-to-do brother of Jeremiah and provider for the entire family. He was against bigamy. Moreover, he claimed to know the cause of the "illness" or the "curse" that descended on Jeremiah's household; he also knew the remedy. According to Babamukuru, Jeremiah's children had been dying because he had been living in sin with Shingayi. They needed to be properly married in church. Jeremiah never questioned any decisions his brother made on his behalf, so he agreed to have a church wedding. His brother would pay all the expenses. Nobody asked Shingayi what she thought about the whole idea. Everything she needed for the wedding was provided. She was measured for her dress and veil. On the wedding day, she was dressed up and taken to the church. Photographs were taken; cake and other refreshments were served. She participated in all the activities but she didn't speak though she was burning with anger inside. After nineteen years of marriage, with a daughter ready to enter college, Shingayi was declared legally married by the patron of her family, her brother-in-law.

But nothing changed in her family except that her brother-in-law had given them his house as a wedding present and Shingayi might stop sleeping on a mat on the dirt floor of her smoky kitchen. She had a baby boy after her wedding; but she remained glum and pessimistic to the end of her life. In a way, Shingayi's life was taken from her at the age of fifteen because of one fatal error-premarital pregnancy. Her partner in "crime" Jeremiah didn't suffer any shame or embarrassment. In fact, he blamed her for ruining his life. So, every endeavor that Shingayi made for the rest of her life was geared towards securing her place as a legitimate wife. In order to do that, she had to swallow all kinds of impositions from her husband and from her brother-in-law. For instance, Babamukuru was determined to pull Jeremiah and his family out of poverty, so he came up with his plan without first discussing it with Jeremiah and his wife. He told Jeremiah he would take his only son Nhamo to live with him and his family at the mission where he was the headmaster. There, Nhamo would have a comfortable life and a good education. With a good education he would get a good job, make good money and improve the lives of his parents and siblings. Both brothers agreed to have Nhamo move to the mission. Shingayi was told of the arrangement; she didn't want her son out of her sight but she dared not breathe a word of dissent in the presence of Babamukuru. She allowed her anger and resentment to consume her silently.

Unfortunately the plan to raise Jeremiah's family through his son aborted with Nhamo's sudden death after barely a couple of years at the mission. Shingayi who was pregnant at the time was devastated; Maiguru, the wife of Babamukuru comforted her as best she could: "You must endure his passing as you endured his coming." She moaned, "I cannot endure it. I too am going to die." After a reasonable length of time following Nhamo's death, Babamukuru came back to Jeremiah with the same idea of elevating his family's living standard. With Nhamo gone, Babamukuru lamented: "It's unfortunate that there is no male child to take this duty, to take this job of raising the family from hunger." Jeremiah agreed with his brother and added: "Tambudzai's sharpness with her books is no use because in the end it will benefit strangers." Nonetheless, he would break tradition and give a girl a chance to step into a man's role for some time before she went on to play her role as a wife. He called his brother and told him about his latest decision for his family: "Er-this girl-heyo, Tambudzai—must be given the opportunity to do what she can for the family before she goes into her husband's home." Even though Tambu wasn't even engaged nor was she thinking about marriage, her father was going to use that inevitable marriage for girls, to deprive her of a good education.

Shingayi was grief-stricken when her husband told her what their patron had decided for their daughter. For the first time, she raised hell! She raised her voice to her husband asking him:

"You, Jeremiah, are you mad? Have you eaten some wild shrub that has gone to your head? I think so, otherwise how could you stand there and tell me to send my child to a place of death, the place where my first living child died! Today you are raving! She will not go. Unless you want me to die too. The anxiety will kill me. I will not let her go."

She got nowhere with her feeble outburst. She became ill immediately; she could not eat or move about. She could not take care of herself and her younger children. But Tambu who was overjoyed, felt triumphant and started packing her bag for the mission. Her mother's condition continued to deteriorate to the point that she thought her mother would die before she left for the mission. Shingayi never fully recovered physically and otherwise for each time she felt that she and Jeremiah were in peace, Babamukuru would come up with yet another plan for her family.

The final blow from Babamukuru's generosity to Shingayi came when her daughter told her that her uncle had decided to send her to a Catholic mission school run by white nuns. She sighed bitterly; she was afraid of the outcome of such an education for her daughter. It would change her daughter into a white person in her manners and speech. She imagined the distance it would create between her and her daughter; it would even cut Tambu from her African roots. With a heavy heart she addressed her daughter:

"Tell me, Tambudzai, does that man want to kill me with his kindness, fattening my children only to take them away like cattle for slaughter? Truly that man is calling down a curse of bad luck on my head. You have survived the mission now he must send you even further away. I've had enough of that man dividing me from my children and ruling my life. He says this and we jump. To wear a veil at my age, to wear a veil! Just imagine-to wear a veil. If I were a witch I would enfeeble his mind . . ."

Shingayi reacted to the latest plan for her daughter in her usual manner—she became ill. This time she became totally helpless; she neglected her newborn son who almost died from diarrhea if Lucia had not come to take care of her sister and her baby.

Throughout her life Shingayi was victimized by womanbeing whose burden she bore in silence. She never made any effort to reclaim her self. Even when Lucia offered to remove her from Jeremiah's home to their fatherland, Shingayi could not make up her mind one way or the other. It was Tambu who explained why her mother could never make up her mind: "Since for most of her life my mother's mind, belonging first to her father and then to her husband, had not been hers to make up, she was finding it difficult to come to a decision." As Lucia continued to press her for an answer, Shingayi sighed and proceeded to give a summary of her dead-but-living condition:

Why do you keep bothering me with this question? Does it matter what I want? Since when has it mattered what I want? Why should it start mattering now? Do you think I wanted to be impregnated by that old dog? Do you think I wanted to travel this far to live in dirt and poverty? Do you really think I wanted the child for whom I made the journey to die only five years after it left the womb? Or my son to be taken from me? So what difference does it make whether I have a wedding or whether I go? It is all the same. What I have endured for nineteen years I can endure for another nineteen, and nineteen more if need be.

Maiguru, the wife of Babamukuru is a classic case of "Appearance is deceitful." She was so good at presenting herself as the happy-go-lucky wife that young Tambudzai saw her as the type of wife that every girl should aspire to become. It was Maiguru's demeanor that made Tambu dismiss her own mother's description of womanhood as false. There was no way being a woman could be a burden as her mother claimed. Maiguru's life with her husband negated everything her mother said. She was a lady of leisure, rich, well-kempt, had a house maid and a demigod of a husband who took good care of her; he drove her in his car wherever she wanted to go. Thus, after examining everything that came with being in Maiguru's position, Tambu decided it was better to be like Maiguru, who was not poor and had not been crushed by the weight of womanhood. Realizing that it was her education that made Maiguru's position possible, eight-year old Tambu announced to her parents, "I shall go to school again." She would cultivate her own piece of ground, grow her own maize and raise the fees for her education.

Tambu lived under this illusion of her aunt until she went to live with her and her family at the Mission. She was overwhelmed and bedazzled by the affluence and polished manner of her aunt and her family. She couldn't believe that what she saw was real. Tambu was too busy adjusting to her own Cinderella-and-the Prince situation to notice that her aunt was a different woman underneath the contented wife she knew. Once in a while she would find herself questioning some puzzling behavior of her aunt: Maiguru, always smiling, always happy, was another puzzle. True, she had good reason to be content. She was Babamukuru's wife. She lived in a comfortable home and was a teacher. She was grateful for all these blessings, but I thought even the saints in heaven must grow disgruntled sometimes and let the lesser angels know. I thought Maiguru deserved to be beatified. She was occasionally upset but never angry. She might be disappointed at times but she was never discouraged.

Tambu instinctively felt that something must be wrong somewhere. Why didn't her aunt have friends to keep company with? Perhaps it was because the other wives didn't have as much education as her aunt. Her aunt had a Bachelor of Arts Degree and she had heard that she even had a Master's Degree in Philosophy, but she didn't believe it. One day she summoned the courage to ask her aunt: "Do you really have a Master's Degree?" "Didn't you know?" Maiguru replied, quite flattered. Tambu was disappointed that her aunt never said anything about it. She had thought that she went to look after her uncle in London as people made her understand. Maiguru went on to clarify things a little for Tambu. Yes, she and her husband had studied in South Africa for their Bachelors and had gone to England for their Master's. Though Maiguru sounded happy as she talked, Tambu perceived the pain in her voice.

It was as if Maiguru had been waiting for somebody to ask the questions that Tambu was now asking her. Therefore, she decided to let it all out. She went on to tell Tambu what contributions she had made toward her husband becoming the benevolent patriarch he was for his siblings and their own families. Her husband and her entire family-in-law had not supported her to continue for a higher degree but now they all were benefiting from her hard work without even giving her any credit for her contributions. She and Tambu had the following conversation:

"Your uncle wouldn't be able to do half the things he does if I didn't work as well."

"You must earn a lot of money." Her aunt said she never received her salary.

"What happens to your money? The money that you earn, does the government take it?

"You could say that." It was too complicated to explain to young Tambu. So, Maiguru tried a subtle explanation. Sighing, she continued:

What it is, to have to choose between self and security. When I was in England I glimpsed for a little while the things I could have been, the things I could have done if-if-if things-were-different-But there was Babawa Chido and the children and the family. And does anyone realize, does anyone appreciate, what sacrifices were made? As for me, no one even thinks about the things I gave up. But that's how it goes, Sisi

Tambu! And when you have a good man and lovely children, it makes it all worthwhile.

And one would ask, "What type of security would a person with a Master's Degree in Philosophy and working at a good job need?" Yet, Security, which for the African woman meant having a husband and children, was the paramount choice for Maiguru. This type of security was defined and proscribed by her culture. As for Maiguru's self, it never featured in her state of wifehood. At marriage, her self was signed over to her husband. Maiguru put self side by side with security because she was educated and knew that maintaining one's self should not be negotiated. However, as a woman, no amount of education could prevent her from choosing that supreme cultural value-security over self. Needless to say, Maiguru's choice came with a price despite her debonair attitude towards her predicament.

Tambu was incredulous that her aunt did not even touch, let alone decide what to do with the money she earned. Worse still, marriage had prevented her from doing the things she wanted to do. Though Tambu genuinely felt sorry for Maiguru, she also felt that since she was the wife of Babamukuru, the sacrifices she made for that position were justified. Thus, Tambu reasoned: "If it was necessary to efface yourself, as Maiguru did so well that you couldn't be sure that she didn't enjoy it, if it was necessary to efface yourself in order to preserve his sense of identity and value, then, I was sure, Maiguru had taken the correct decisions. To Tambu's way of seeing things, it was necessary for a wife to "kill" her self in order to preserve the sense of identity and value of her husband.

Maiguru's ultimate sacrifice was giving up her identity to be swallowed by her husband's. Maiguru succeeded in making everyone believe that she enjoyed living her dead life. She was not at all a lady of leisure, as outsiders believed; she worked at a salaried job and she worked like any other wife to run her house. Though she had a maid, she did most of the grocery and other shopping. These were very frustrating to her because she depended on the good will of her husband to drive her to places. Once she hinted that she couldn't get her chores done because she had no transportation; her daughter, Nyasha snapped at her and told her to learn to drive. She retorted, "And where do you think I would get the car from? Do you think I can afford to buy one?" And this from a salaried lady with a Master's Degree in Philosophy! At the dinner table, she waited on her husband like a paid servant. She sweet-talked and baby-talked to him; she made sure that everyone tiptoed around the house to avoid getting on her husband's delicate nerves. She was forever watchful over her husband's comfort, so, she anticipated his every wish and ministered to him.

On countless occasions, she sat helpless as her husband literally fought their daughter and tried to beat the girl's self out of her. On the last physical fight between daughter and father, when the former punched the latter in the face, Maiguru could only weakly try to hold her husband back with the help of her son. When her husband insisted that he would kill Nyasha and hang himself, Maiguru started crying:

"No, Babawa Chido, kani. If you must kill somebody, kill me. But my daughter, no, leave her alone. Please, I beg you, leave her alone." Her husband paid no attention to her; he was determined to make Nyasha obey him. She must become the type of daughter he wanted her to be. He never let up till he drove his daughter to a psychiatric hospital.

The most embarrassing aspect of Maiguru's dead-but-alive situation was her lack of participation in decision-making in matters affecting her and other family members. She was never consulted by her husband in anything he did on behalf of the families of his siblings. On the two occasions when he decided to bring Nhamo and then Tambu to come and live with them at the mission, Babamukuru did not discuss the matter with his wife. Yet, he knew it would be his wife's responsibility to take care of these children as she did her own children. As a well-to-do eldest son, Babamukuru instituted a family reunion with his siblings and their children every Christmas in their village home. This was one way of bringing an occasional happiness to his people. The narrator observed that Babamukuru always provided not only the Christmas meal, but also Christmas itself for as many of the clan that gathered for as long as they gathered. At one such occasion, he demonstrated how he unilaterally made decisions affecting the entire family members. He had to provide for twenty-four members of his extended family, plus several uninvited members of his clan for two weeks. He never considered the logistics of going to the river to fetch water for cooking and laundry and bathing for all these people. He did not consider that firewood had to be fetched to supplement the small Dutch stove owned by his wife. Yet, he did not discuss anything with his wife whose responsibility it was to delegate and supervise these chores. He knew that his wife would be doing most of the cooking still, he did not consult her on the quantity of food items to buy, especially perishable items like meat and vegetables. Therefore, when he brought home half of an ox for Christmas, his wife started grumbling. The narrator noted that Maiguru might have disagreed with her husband on another matter if not, it was unusual for her to grumble.

Maiguru can only grumble about having to go along with her husband's decisions. Under normal circumstances she should be the one to decide what and how much would be needed to feed their family crowd. He was irritated by her grumbling because he felt that she wanted him to fail in his duty as provider. Maiguru pointed out however:

"A whole ox would be too much. Even a side is too much. But what I object to is the way everybody expects me to spend all my time cooking for them. When you provide so much food, then I end up slaving for everybody."

Babamukuru dismissed her flimsy excuse but reminded her that she had all the girls and other women to help her, if that was her only reason for objecting to the quantity of meat. The narrator comments:

So Maguru, Nyasha, the three helping girls and myself were on our feet all day. Maiguru worked harder than anybody else, because as the senior wife and owner of the best cooking facilities as well as provider of the food to cook, she was expected to oversea all the culinary operations. It was a ceaseless work and unwise to delegate because she had to make sure that the food lasted until the end of the vacation.

Unlike most educated married African women, Maiguru stooped too low for a lady of her rank and because of that, her husband and other family members wiped their feet on Maiguru and she took it "cheerfully?" For instance, when the meat spoiled and turned green, her sister-in-law blamed her and insulted her by showing her the chewed rotten meat she spat out of her mouth and suggested that Maiguru be more responsible in future. The comment and the gesture threw Maiguru into a dreadful panic. She took to cooking, twice a day, a special pot of refrigerated meat for the patriarchy to eat as they planned and constructed the family's future. A normal educated married African woman would not tolerate the type of blatant insults that Maiguru received from her husband and families-in-law. But Maiguru would withdraw into her womanbeing and work herself to exhaustion in order please everyone around her.

After remaining on her feet all day Maiguru was tired and wanted to go to bed and sleep. She did not wish to join the other women protesting their exclusion from a meeting that focused on Lucia, the wild female. "I don't want to intrude into the affairs of my husband's family. I shall just keep quiet and go to bed," she said. On reaching the door she curtseyed and asked in a respectful voice, "May I pass?" Her husband couldn't believe her "rudeness;" he reprimanded her sternly and in a firm voice said: "Ma'Chido, we are listening to a very important case here. Sit down and listen with us." She steeled herself and asked in a fake playful voice, "Could it be that important? We did not know anything about it." He insisted: "Ma'Chido I have invited you to sit down and listen to this case." She obeyed and sat on the floor. This time the sister-in-law who had insulted her came to her defense, saying to her brother: "I am sure it is not necessary, Maiguru works very hard all day. Maybe it is best for her to sleep." The brother-in-law joined his sister to plead for Maiguru: "She is so tired, too tired even to sit and listen. But it is true. Maiguru works hard. Ya, she really works hard to keep things comfortable here." Her husband, secretly enjoying the praise his wife received added irritably: "If she is tired, why doesn't she say so?" Then he granted her permission to leave.

The above incidents are just a few to show the extent to which an educated married woman was treated as a servant and a child. Her husband got angry with her because she dared to grumble when she was expected to shut her mouth and not question decisions on things that concerned her directly. She was constantly expected to go along with decisions that went against her better judgment. She suffered all this because it was her responsibility to make sure her prop helped secure her husband firmly on that high chair of authority that his society hoisted him. She had to deny herself everything that defined her as an independent thinking person, to make her husband's manhood shine.

There is nothing more oppressive to an individual than living a lie. More often than not, the truth would explode in the face of that individual even at the last minute of life. Maiguru lived so long with a false picture she presented to people that she had to explode to allow the truth about her true self to emerge. It happened when Lucia, a charity case in Maiguru's house "rode slip shod" into her living room and demanded to speak to her husband alone. The way Lucia charged into the room convinced Maiguru that something must be wrong, so she inquired in her gentle manner:

"What is wrong, Mainini? I see you are upset"

"Don't worry yourself, Maiguru. The matter concerns Babamukuru."

"Are you sure, Mainin?"

"I am sure, Maiguru."

"You can't talk to no one but Babawa Chido?"

"No one but Babamukuru."

Maiguru left Lucia in the living room and went away to wait for her husband's return. When he finally came home Lucia told him to his face that he had been wrong in the severe punishment he had given Tambudzai for not attending her mother's wedding. Babamukuru was impressed with Lucia's boldness but didn't show it. He explained that Tambudzai had no right to disobey his orders, especially since she was a girl. He added by way of stressing the seriousness of Tambu's offense, "My wife here would not have disobeyed me in the way that Tambudzai did." Bold Lucia shut back:

"Well, Babamukuru, maybe when you marry a woman, she is obliged to obey you. But some of us aren't married, so we don't know how to do it. That is why I have been able to tell you frankly what is in my heart." Babamukuru applauded Lucia when she left the room and turning to his wife he chuckled: "That one, she is like a man herself." Babamukuru admired and applauded an unmarried younger woman for challenging his authority, yet he couldn't stand his wife grumbling at his unilateral decisions in all family matters.

Still nursing the insult from Lucia, Maiguru let go her pent-up anger and vented it on her husband for the first time in their married years:

Babawa Chido, I am tired of my house being a hotel for your family. I am tired of being a housekeeper for them. I am tired of being nothing in a home I am working myself sick to support. And now that Lucia can walk in here and tell me that the things she discusses with you, here in my house, are none of my business. I am sick of it Babawa Chido. Let me tell you, I have had enough!

Babamukuru was unbelieving. The children who were eavesdropping didn't know how to interpret the commotion because they had never heard the couple quarrel before.

Babamukuru tried to remain calm and to tell his wife soothingly that her words were not good; that what she was saying was not true. She spoke clearly and said that bad situations called for bad words and bad things were happening to her in her home. "No, Ma' Chido, it is not as you say, he said softly. But Maiguru would not be pacified any more so she flared up: "It is as I say. And when I keep quiet you think I am enjoying it. So today I am telling you I am not happy. I am not happy any more in this house."

He snapped at her: "Then go where you will be happy."

Maiguru took the challenge and her daughter and her niece waited anxiously for her next move. The narrator observes:

To our surprise, Maiguru did leave, by bus, early the next morning. She did not slink away in the dark, but quite openly packed a suitcase, put on her travelling clothes, had her breakfast and left.

Maiguru's daughter was highly impressed and happy for her mother but Tambu thought of Maiguru's leaving as an abrupt abandonment of her daughter. However, Nyasha saw the difference between people deserting their daughters and people saving themselves. Yes, Maiguru's leaving was truly a gesture of self-saving. Whereas Tambu only thought in terms of the huge housekeeping problems that Maiguru's leaving would cause, Nyasha only thought in terms of her mother's emancipation and was comforted by it. Nyasha strongly identified with her mother's entrapment because she was entrapped by her father's iron rule. She was comforted because she now knew that breaking free was possible, she would wait her turn to do the same.

Maiguru's leaving demonstrated that she still had determination and resolve. She had taken the first step to liberation. The crucial question remained, would she from now on, hold on to her womanself and allow it to supplant her womanbeing? Only her future actions could answer this question. And the reader gets a glimpse of her future actions through the speculation of her daughter and niece who knew her best. True, Maiguru has broken free, but she had gone to her brother's! And when Nyasha heard it she gasped, "A man! She always runs to men. There's no hope." The problem is not really running to her brother or to any other man. The fundamental question is, where would she ultimately end up as a decision-making self? The girls toyed with different options of what she could become and where she could go to achieve total freedom and self fulfillment. In the end, reality set in and the girls recalled that Maiguru's dead-but-alive condition was too deep to be routed by a resuscitated fragile self. They knew that even if there were extraordinary options and endless places to break out to, Maiguru might choose neither.

It was a sad truth, tragic in Maiguru's case, because even if there had been somewhere to go, she would not have been able to, since her investment, in the form of her husband and two children, was all at the mission. Consequently, after five days, Maiguru telephoned her house and left a message with her son Chido, telling him where she was. Chido passed the message to Nyasha, who, with a heavy heart, passed it on to her father. Although it was late at night, Babamukuru jumped into his car to go and retrieve his prodigal wife.

Certainly, Maiguru made some tiny gains in her relationship with her husband. She also showed changes in her attitude towards him. Tambu remarked the positive changes. For instance, she smiled more often and less mechanically. She fussed less over the girls and more willing to talk about sensible things and although she still called Babamukuru her daddy sweet, most of her baby-talk had disappeared. As far as Nyasha was concerned: "It's such a waste. Imagine what she might have been with the right kind of exposure."

Most importantly, Maiguru's temporary break had some positive impact on her husband. He now reluctantly asked her opinion before making an important decision. For instance, Tambu gained admission with a scholarship, to an all girls' Catholic secondary school. Babamukuru felt she had had enough education; she should start working and get married. In the presence of his wife he told Tambu what he was planning for her. Then, for the first time in their marriage, he turned to his wife and asked: "Mai, is there anything that you would wish to say?" Ever so softly Maiguru answered: "Yes, Baba." Visibly startled, Babamukuru exclaimed: "You do!" He recovered his composure and invited her to," "speak freely, Mai. Say whatever you are thinking." Maiguru went on to remind him that their people were prejudiced against educated women. She reminded him of how everybody was against her own education. She discussed all the arguments her husband laid out against further education for Tambu. Then she concluded that her husband's excuses for holding Tambu back were very weak. Tambu should be allowed to go. To further testify to the impact of Maiguru's leaving, Babamukuru also turned to Tambu and tentatively asked if she had anything to say. In the end he took Tambu to the village for Christmas, and told her father: "I have decided to let her go." Tambu attributed her uncle's change of heart to Maiguru's speech and intervention on her behalf.

But, as long as Maiguru had her investment-husband and children-to take care of, it remains doubtful that she would gain total freedom to do as she pleased. It is doubtful that she would not relapse into dead-but-living condition from time to time, if not completely.

THREE DEAD-LIVING WOMEN

In Toni Morrison's *Song of Solomon*, we encounter Ruth Forster Dead and her two daughters, Magdalene and First Corinthians Dead. These three women are the most dead of all dead-but-living women in black women's novels. Looking back at the history of their last name, it seemed as if the drunken Yankee anticipated the entry of these women into the Dead family when he messed up the last name of the first Macon in 1869

The first indication of the dead-but-living condition of these women was in reference to how different groups of women reacted to Milkman, Ruth's son. The women who did not hate Ruth saw her son as dull. Those who hated her saw her son as peculiar. Others considered him deep, even mysterious. It was this last group who saw that Ruth's house was more prison than palace; that the Dodge sedan was for Sunday drives only. And these women felt sorry for Ruth Foster and her dry daughters.

From this weird reference to Ruth and her daughters, the reader is led into their prison home where they were terrorized and subjected to perpetual hate and emotional crippling by Macon Dead, the husband of Ruth and father of their children. To his family, Macon was like a rumbling volcano whose unpredictable eruptions spilled lava of hate, anger and fear on his family members:

Macon kept each member of his family awkward with fear. His hatred of his wife glittered and sparked in every word he spoke to her. The disappointment he felt with his daughters sifted down on them like ash, dulling their buttery complexions and choking the lilt out of what should have been girlish voices . . . The way he mangled their grace, wit and self-esteem, was the single excitement of their days. Without the tension and drama he ignited, they might not have known what to do with themselves . . . and his wife, Ruth, began her days stunned into stillness by her husband's contempt and ended them wholly animated by it.

Macon's hate for his wife found backing in what he wrongly assumed happened earlier in their marriage. But how does one explain his hate for his daughters? What did these innocent girls do to merit such deadly hate from their father? There's no indication in the novel that the girls did something wrong on their own to alienate their father. The slight hint of their vicarious wrongdoing came from Macon's suspicion that Dr. Foster, their grandfather, might have fathered them. But Macon dismissed that notion when he figured out that Dr. Foster was impotent. So, one plausible explanation of Macon's disgust with his daughters is simply the issue of gender. That they were girls was reason enough to earn his hate. If that's not a plausible explanation, why did he not extend the same feeling of hate and shabby treatment to his son? Macon tolerated Milkman and was eager to train him in the business of "owning things" because Milkman was not a girl. In fact, this idea of gender discrimination is supported by a remark made by Guitar, Milkman's friend. For instance, when Guitar told Milkman that everybody, except black men, wanted black people dead, Milkman countered with, "Then why did my father-who is a very black man-try to kill me before I was even born?" Guitar replied, "Maybe he thought you were a little girl . . ." Thus, Guitar's remark provides, not only a partial explanation of Macon's utter disregard for female members of his household, it also speaks directly to this universal victimization of women that Dangarembga spoke about in *Nervous Conditions*. This victimization did not depend on culture or race; it didn't depend on lack of education or poverty or anything tangible. Men took it everywhere with them. Even heroes like Babamukuru did it. Even young male children like Milkman victimized their female siblings and their mothers. Taking the cue from his father, Milkman walked all over his sisters and his mother. And because he always looked past the faces of his sisters, he had never been able to really distinguish them or their roles from his mother.

Milkman didn't have normal sibling relationship with his sisters, not because they were much older by thirteen and twelve years respectively, but because he had that "God-given-right that all men are supposed to have over women." Milkman exercised that right when he told his father that Corinthians was secretly seeing Henry Porter. When Lena asked why he did such a spiteful thing, he replied, "I had to. I'd love for her to find somebody, but I know that man . . . And I don't think he . . ." Lena furiously burst out:

What do you know about somebody not being good enough for somebody else? And since when did you care whether

Corinthians stood up or fell down. You've been laughing at us all your life. Corinthians, Mama. Me. Using us, ordering us, and judging us: how we cook your food; how we keep your house. But now all of a sudden you have Corinthians' welfare at heart and break her up from a man you don't approve of . . . Where do you get the right to decide our lives? I'll tell you where. From that hog's gut that hangs down between your legs.

Once again, it is the question of maleness versus femaleness. Femaleness as opposed and inferior to maleness, as Dangarembga expressed it. Milkman's maleness gave him the right to interfere in his sisters' lives.

Macon provided free room and board and pocket money for his grown up daughters. They both went to school and Corinthians was even sent to France for part of her education. Magdalene would later reveal to Milkman why she didn't go to college. "I didn't go to college because of him (her father). Because I was afraid of what he might do to Mama. What could Macon have done to Ruth? Murder her? He probably could have. After all, didn't he commit his first murder at sixteen? Didn't he always regret not killing Ruth when he felt he had a justifiable reason to do so? He sent his daughters to school, but what use was their education to them or to anybody else? Is there a more cruel way of punishing an educated person than preventing her from using her learning in a meaningful and self-fulfilling way? With all their education, Macon's daughters ended up in their prison home, too good for anything or for anybody. Corinthians priced herself out of the marriage market with her refinement and French touch. Educated women of her type intimidated professional black men. Even ordinary blue-collar workers wouldn't take her when she passed middle age. In short, Magdalene and Corinthians became old maids. They kept quiet and busy, making artificial red-velvet roses, dead roses that became an extension of their dead selves. Corinthians hated that stupid hobby and would give any excuse to avoid them because the roses spoke to her of death. They reminded her of Mr. Smith jumping to his death and their velvet roses flying all over the snow covered ground when their mother in shock, dropped the bucket filled with roses. She also associated the artificial roses with her own death, because, if she didn't break away from them, she would surely die making roses.

It was this morbid thought that sent the forty-four year old Corinthians groveling before Henry Porter, a yardman and a tenant of her father's, a drunken man who urinated from an attic window over the heads of a crowd. She was begging him to take her to his one-room apartment in his borrowed rickety Oldsmobile car. But after she slighted Henry and he was about to leave her, she realized he was her first and perhaps the last chance for going to bed with a man. So, she lay on the hood of Henry's car, banging her knuckles till they ached. She was ready to smash her fist through the windscreen just to feel his warm flesh. After all, he was the only thing that could protect her from a smothering death of dry roses.

Macon denied his daughters a healthy nurturing home. He killed their girlhood, their adolescence and their adulthood by preventing them from mixing and interacting with people their own age. On the pretext of saving them from the company of their social inferiors, he frightened away young men who could have come calling. In the end, his daughters boiled dry from years of yearning. In their forties, the daughters were literally remanded to their rooms from whose windows they looked at life roll by. Like incarcerated criminals, they had to find something to occupy their hands. That was how Lena came up with making roses. She told Milkman "I was the one who started making artificial roses. Not Mama. Not Corinthians. Me. I loved to do it. It kept me quiet." She compared this activity with those of inmates of an asylum, who weave baskets and make rag rugs. It keeps them quiet. Like those inmates, they had to keep busy or else, they would figure out that something was wrong, and they could do something terrible to upset the "system" set up by their father.

The Dead family house was hell for these three women. Their cat-and-mouse relationship with Macon pushed the limits of human endurance. Like mice and cat, the women could only relax in Macon's absence but they waited eagerly for any hint of him. A normal family activity like diner was stressful, especially for Ruth who received only criticism for her cooking and sometimes beatings for her manners. Ruth and her children served as part of Macon's property and he paraded them as such. For instance, when Lena was warning Milkman to stay out of Corinthian's business, she told him of an incident that took place before he was born:

When we were little girls, before you were born, he took us to the icehouse once. Drove us there in his Hudson. We were all dressed up . . . There were other children there. Barefoot, naked to the waist, dirty. But we stood apart, near the car, in white stockings, ribbons, and gloves. And when he talked to the men, he kept glancing at us, us and the car. The car and us. You see, he took us there so they could see us, envy us, envy him.

Macon did not take his little girls to have fun eating ice with other children in the community. He did not want his children interacting with "dirty" kids of the community. Lena went on to narrate what happened when they all tried to be children:

Then one of the little boys came over to us and put his hand on Corinthian's hair. She offered him her piece of ice and before we knew it, he was running toward us. He knocked the ice out of Corinthian's hand into the dirt and shoved us both into the car.

First he displayed us, then he splayed us. All our lives were like that: he would parade us like virgins through Babylon, then humiliate us like whores in Babylon. Now he has knocked the ice out of Corinthian's hand again. And you are to blame.

Figuratively Macon knocked the ice out of Corinthians' hand again when he literally put her under house arrest to prevent any further interaction between her and Henry Porter: He has forbidden her to leave the house, made her quit her job, evicted the man, garnished his wages . . .

The weighty inhumanity of Macon's act of cutting Corinthians down can only be felt by recalling what Corinthians went through to arrive at the point where her father pushed her "back into the grave." At forty-two, Corinthians suffered a severe depression when she woke up to the fact that she might spend her entire life making roses. Miraculously her womanself crawled out and pushed her out of the house to find some meaning to life. Twenty-one years after graduation from college, Corinthians swallowed her shallow pride, disguised herself and went in search of job. She could only find the one job reserved for colored girls of any background-domestic work. Her main problem was keeping the nature of her job a secret from her family. Her education served her well when she used the word amanuensis to describe her job at Michael-

Mary Graham's home. Her mother was impressed by the Latin word she didn't understand, but she made sure to flabbergast her guests with it when they came to tea. Corinthians devised ingenious ways to keep her disguise in place for two years. The opportunity to get out of the house alone and take a bus to her job, gave her a sense of purpose and achievement. Besides, it brought her in contact with other maids though she kept her distance and showed off her learning and refinement. Most importantly, it brought her in contact with Henry Porter, a man who paid attention to her, admired her and eventually became her lover. After her first time in bed with Henry she felt easy:

In place of vanity she now felt a self-esteem that was quite new. She was grateful to him, this man who rented a room from her father, who ate with a knife and did not even own a pair of dress shoes. A perfect example of the men her parents had kept her from (and whom she had also kept herself from) all her life because such a man was known to beat his woman, betray her, and leave her.

It was while she was relishing her new-found-freedom, albeit secretly, that Milkman "poured sand into her rice," ruining everything. Her emerging womanself was nipped and it would likely shrivel to its root. Knowing how deeply Macon's hate and determination can run, it is unlikely that Corinthians would be let out of that house again. And it is doubtful that she would find the courage once more to break out of her prison. As for her sister, Lena, she had already resigned herself to the fate of making those dead roses to the end of her days.

The Sunday family ride in Macon's Packard was no occasion for family fun or quality time. Like everything else, the ride was mainly for Macon's self-aggrandizement.

71

He needed to impress the black community with his wealth and provoke their jealousy. For Ruth, the ride was a way for her to show off her family. For the young boy, the ride was a burden since he had to be wedged between his parents, facing backwards in order to see. Only the daughters seemed to derive some joy from the outing. It was their only adventure, the time they could sit back and watch men and women go by. All normal activities associated with car rides were denied Macon's car. Even a normal conversation between family members was strained. As the daughters tried to force a conversation, Macon ignored them. When Ruth tried to assert herself into the conversation, by commenting on her husband's driving, Macon snapped at her: "If you say one more thing to me about the way I drive, you're going to walk back home. I mean it." And like the family's huge house, the Packard had no real lived life at all. So they called it Macon Dead's hearse.

Eating together at the diner table is an occasion that most families appreciate. For the Dead family, especially for Ruth, diner time was froth with danger. It was a time for Ruth to sit on the edge of her chair waiting nervously for Macon's criticisms and humiliations. During one of these tempestuous diner sessions, we witnessed the saddest dramatic scene in the novel. Ruth was narrating what she considered a funny anecdote. It was about her participation in a Catholic Mass at a wedding that she attended. Her daughters were listening with some interest while Milkman was only half listening. When Ruth ended her story, Macon was furious and this exchange took place:

"You didn't know that only Catholics take communion in a Catholic Church?"

"No, Macon. How would I know?"

"You see them put up their own school, keep their kids out of public schools, and you still think their religious stuff is open to anybody who wants to drop in?"

"Communion is communion."

"You're a silly woman."

"Father Padrew didn't think so."

"You made a fool of yourself."

"Mrs. Djvorak didn't think so."

"She was just trying to keep the wedding going, keep you from fucking it up."

"Macon, please don't use that language in front of the children."

"What goddam children? Everybody in here is old enough to vote."

"There is no call for an argument."

"You make a fool of yourself in a Catholic Church, embarrass everybody at the reception, and come to the table to gloat about how wonderful you were?"

"Macon . . ."

"And sit down there lying, saying you didn't know any better?"

"Anna Dvjorak wasn't the least bit—"

"Anna Djvorak don't even know your name! She called you Dr. Foster's daughter! I bet you one hundred dollars she still don't know your name! You by yourself ain't nobody. You your daddy's daughter!"

"That's so, I certainly am my daddy's daughter."

Macon dropped his fork and smashed his fist into Ruth's jaw, wiping out her smile. Before his father could draw his hand back, Milkman had yanked him by the back of his coat collar, up out of his chair, and knocked him into the radiator. "You touch her again, one more time, and I'll kill you," Milkman said to his father. Macon was more shocked than humiliated by his son's defensive gesture over his mother. In all his prosperous years, Macon had presumed himself impregnable but Milkman's reaction awakened him. Later, he tried to explain to his son, the origin of his passionate hatred for his wife. He went back to when he married her in 1917; she was only sixteen. He wasn't in love with her, besides, marriage didn't require love then. He told his son about the disgusting practice of Dr. Foster delivering Ruth's daughters. When he protested Ruth and her father ignored him. Furthermore, he had married Ruth with the hope that her father would help finance his Real Estate business. But his efforts to borrow money from Dr. Foster failed. When he asked his wife to speak to her father on his behalf, Ruth said it had to be her father's decision, that she couldn't influence him. "Then I began to wonder who she was married to—me or him," he said. From that point on, Macon developed the notion that Ruth and her father had an incestuous relationship all their lives. His suspicions were confirmed, he claimed to Milkman, when he surprised Ruth in bed with her dead father. "In the bed. That's where she was when I opened the door. Laying next to him. Naked as a yard dog, kissing him. Him dead and white and puffy and skinny, and she had his fingers in her mouth." From that incident, his suspicion became so intense that he imagined Dr. Foster had fathered his own grand daughters. Though he dismissed the idea when he found that that bastard couldn't fuck nothing, yet there's lots of things a man can do to please a woman, even if he can't fuck. Macon still wondered what went on between father and daughter, for, if Ruth could be kissing her dead father, "what'd she do when he was alive?" The best thing would have been to kill a woman who committed such an odious act, he thought. "I swear, many's the day I regret she talked me out of killing her," he told his son. Thus, the root cause of Macon's hellish hatred and spite for his wife was the nagging suspicion that his wife and her father carried on an incestuous relationship. To add to that, Macon despised his father-in-law for his refusal to lend him any financial support for his business. In fact, Ruth reasoned that Macon didn't kill her because he needed her money. She told her son, "I guess my father's money was more important to him than the satisfaction of killing me."

For the entire length of the novel, Ruth Foster Dead was a dead-but-living woman. For nearly twenty years Macon starved his wife of sex; he felt neither guilt nor remorse because he never loved her to begin with. As the author commented: In almost twenty years during which he had not laid eyes on her naked feet, he missed only her underwear. For a person raised in a culture in which sex is a paramount value, sexual starvation is the severest punishment to inflict on a healthy sexual person. Therefore, Macon could not have chosen a worse punishment for Ruth. Except for four consecutive days during which Macon made love to his wife under the spell of Pilate's voodoo, Ruth lived the life of a repudiated wife. Two months after Macon's hypnotic sexual encounter with Ruth, the latter discovered she was pregnant. When Macon learned of it, his anger and hostility were immeasurable. He tried every means possible to have the fetus aborted. He failed and his son was born. Even with the birth of an heir, Macon's loathing and hate for Ruth did not diminish. To deal with the emotional torture, Ruth resorted to sublimation. She continued to breastfeed her son several years beyond the weaning age:

She sat in the room holding her son on her lap, staring at his closed eyelids and listening to the sound of his sucking . . . He was too young to be dazzled by her nipples, but he was old enough to be bored by the flat taste of mother's milk, so he came reluctantly, as to a chore . . . She felt him. His restraint, his courtesy, his indifference, all of which pushed her into fantasy . . .

Ruth could have continued this breastfeeding routine for as long as possible, if Freddie the janitor hadn't surprised her at it and ruined everything. Worse still, it resulted in a permanent change of name for her son, from Macon to Milkman. It equally sent her husband on a rampage of sorts, trying to figure out how the "dirty" name came about, for no one would volunteer the information. It gave him an excuse for renewed outrage and vicious berating of his wife:

Without knowing any of the details, however, he (Macon) guessed, with the accuracy of a mind sharpened by hatred, that the name he heard school children call his son . . . was not clean. It sounded dirty, intimate, and hot. He knew that wherever the name came from, it had something to do with his wife and was, like the emotion he always felt when thinking of her, coated with disgust.

As one would expect, this "misnaming" of his son plunged Macon back to the incident leading to the conception of the unwanted baby. A flash back on his life revealed a change for the better in everything for him, except Ruth. He still wished he had strangled her back in 1921. She hadn't stopped spending occasional nights out of the house, but she was fifty years old now and what lover could she have kept for so long?

Spending occasional nights out of the house was another way of dealing with her abandonment by Macon. She needed to be with someone who cared about her, even if that person was her dead father. Through all those years of her nightly pilgrimage to her father's grave, Macon believed, with some relief, that she was having an affair with some man. It was one more mystery with which Ruth addled his mind. Milkman might have heard of these visits and other unflattering stories about his mother but he never asked her about them. However, after his father told his side of the story, Milkman was poised to find some facts about his mother on his own.

The opportunity came one night that his mother went on her night visit to Fairfield Cemetery. About one-thirty in the morning, Milkman was driving home from a party when he saw his mother walking away from the house. He followed her to the bus stop and saw her get on the bus. Then he followed the bus to its final stop where Ruth disembarked and waited for the train. When she got into the train, Milkman did the same. At Fairfield Cemetery, Ruth got off and made straight for the cemetery. Milkman hid behind a tree to watch her. As Ruth lay prostrate upon her father's grave, Milkman's thoughts raced back to all that his father had told him about his mother: Now he knew, if he'd had any doubts, that all his father had told him was true. She was a silly, selfish, queer, faintly obscene woman. When Ruth came out an hour later, Milkman startled her by suddenly stepping out from behind the tree. She stumbled in alarm and took a great gulp of air into her mouth. As she tried desperately to regain composure, Milkman confronted her: "You come to lay down on your father's grave? Is that what you've been doing all these years? Spending a night every now and then with your father?"

Then Ruth told her own side of the story. She started in mid-sentence:

" . . . because the fact is that I am a small woman . . . I'm small because I was pressed small. I lived in a great big house that pressed me into a small package. I had no friends. But I didn't think I'd ever need a friend because I had him. I was small, but he was big . . . He was not a good man . . . He was an arrogant man, and often a foolish and destructive one. But he cared whether and he cared how I lived, and there was, and is, no one else in the world who ever did. And for that I would do anything."

She then told Milkman how he was conceived and born and how his birth did not mend the rift between her and Macon. She told him how Macon moved out of their bedroom forever and:

"That's the way things stayed until I couldn't stand it anymore. Until I thought I'd really die if I had to live that way. With nobody touching me, or even looking as though they'd like to touch me. That's when I started going to Fairfield. To talk to somebody who wanted to listen and not laugh at me. Somebody I could trust. Somebody who trusted me. Somebody who was . . . interested in me. For my own self. I didn't care if that somebody was under the ground . . . I think I was just afraid I'd die that way . . . Then Pilate came to town."

At the end of his mother's pathetic story, Milkman still needed to verify some other facts. He asked his mother point blank, "Were you in the bed with your father when he was dead? Naked?" Ruth said no. She was in her slip by the bedside and she kissed her father's fingers. Milkman continued:

"You nursed me?"

"Yes."

"Until I was . . . old. Too old."

"And I prayed for you. Every single night and every single day. On my knees. Now you tell me. What harm did I do you on my knees?"

Ruth's loneliness in the midst of her family members is unnerving. She received no affection from anyone, including her son whom she loved with passion; a son for whom she would kill anyone that tried to harm a hair on his head. Even Milkman did not hide his impressions about his mother. For him, she was just there like a fixture. At twenty-two he began to see his mother in a new light. She was a frail woman content to do tiny things; to grow and cultivate small life that would not hurt her if it died. Even when he in righteous anger struck his father to protect his mother, Milkman knew that his chivalric gesture was not driven by filial love. He would not pretend that it was love for his mother. She was too insubstantial, too shadowy for love. Milkman felt he acted like any other man who saw another man hit a helpless person . . . Isn't that what men did, he asked. The fact that the prey and predator were his parents made his act more poignant but it didn't change the facts. His sister Lena had a different explanation for his act. She said:

"You think because you hit him once that we all believe you were protecting her. Taking her side. It's all a lie. You were taking over, letting us know you had the right to tell her and all of us what to do."

To say that Ruth Foster Dead was a dead-but-living woman is an understatement! The author commented on Ruth's attitude towards death:

In a way she was jealous of death. Inside all that grief she felt when the doctor died, there had been a bit of pique too, as though he had chosen a more provocative companion than she was—and had deliberately followed death when it beckoned. She was fierce in the presence of death, heroic even, as she was at no other time. Its threat gave her direction, clarity, audacity.

Ruth saw death as a rival to whom she lost her father. Her desire to have and keep her father explained her bizarre penchant to seek solace and company among the dead. Her husband merely applied the coup de grace to an almost dead wife whose running-battle with death did more to create her dead-but-living condition.

PATRIARCHY BOWS TO WOMANSELF

Through Efuru her heroine, Flora Nwapa portrayed the ultimate charismatic womanself. Efuru's physical, as well as inner beauty charmed people around her. But she did not flaunt her beauty. She understood and respected her culture which she dealt with on her own terms. Efuru was comfortable in her womanhood.

The novel *Efuru*, opens with the heroine Efuru, calmly violating the most sacred symbol of marriage in her culture-bride price. No marriage can take place prior to the settlement of bride price. Efuru fell in love with Adizua, a poverty-stricken, never-do-well fellow. Adizua was very much in love but dared not hope to marry Efuru because he could not afford the bride price for any girl let alone some one with Efuru's beauty and pedigree. Efuru read his mind and decided to do the unthinkable. Efuru sort of eloped because she went ahead to live with Adizua before the bride price was even discussed with her people. Although the young man and his mother were very pleased to have Efuru, they were shocked and frightened by Efuru's unprecedented act. They were particularly worried about the scandal it would cause for Efuru and her highly respected father. While she welcomed Efuru, the future mother-in-law asked, "But your father, what will you say to him?" Efuru answered: "Leave that to me, I shall settle it myself."

Late that evening, a family member went to inform Efuru's worried father: "Efuru has run away to a young man. It is a shame . . . This young man is nobody. His family is not known . . . Something must be done immediately to get her back. Consequently, a team of elders was dispatched to retrieve Efuru. When she saw them, she rushed out to greet them. She explained that her husband had gone to the farm and apologized for his absence. Then she placed before them, the best Kola nuts and the finest homemade gin that money could buy. Efuru radiated such joy and contentment that the team was confused and disarmed. Before they left they said to her: "You seem to be happy here and we wonder why your father wants us to bring you back. We shall tell him what we have seen. But your husband must fulfill the customs of our people. He must see your father. Let him not be afraid." Efuru went down on her knees and thanked them, saying: "Tell my father that I shall be the last person to bring shame on him. My husband is not rich. In fact he is poor. But the bride price must be paid. I must see that it is done." Nobody had ever heard a woman utter such words! Is a woman ever involved in settling her own bride price? But Efuru would be the first woman to take charge of settling her own bride price. Not only that, she would be the one to raise the funds for it! This literally amounted to Efuru marrying herself!

Efuru knew that the fastest way to make money in her town was by trading. She would trade instead of farming along side her husband. She told him: "If you like, go to the farm. I am not cut out for farm work. I am going to trade." This was the second rude shock to Efuru's husband. Adizua went to the farm alone but could get no work done. He would dream all day about his beautiful wife at home. Other men sympathized with Adizua and even had their own fantasies about Efuru. They talked of Efuru's beauty all the time: She is so beautiful. You would think that the woman of the lake is her mother."

In addition to the unpaid bride price, Efuru had to be circumcised in order to be initiated into womanhood. The ceremony involved money, but more importantly, Efuru's father must be told before the ritual is performed. When Adizua reminded her, she once again took charge of the situation. "He won't be told. It will make him angrier. When we have enough money to pay the bride price, we shall approach elderly men who will help us beg him." Efuru went through the ritual bath as the ceremony was called. Instead of three months of confinement in a fattening room, Efuru persuaded her mother-in-law to let her out after one month. She paraded her freshened beauty in the market as tradition demanded. Efuru ignored all gossip about the unpaid bride price and her poor husband.

Adizua could not continue to fool himself after another poor harvest from his farm. Efuru consoled him and he needed very little persuasion to join Efuru in her trading. Within a few months, they made enough money to pay the bride price. Adizua sent word to Efuru's father who was happy to receive them. On the set date, Efuru went to her father's house early in the morning to wait for her husband and his people to arrive in the evening. Her father and his people listened to the apologies and received compensations before the main bride price was negotiated and paid. At the end of the ceremony, Efuru and her husband knelt before her father and received his blessing and advice. They went home and for the first time since that fateful Nkwo day, the two felt really married. Thus, for the first time in the history of Ugwuta people, and indeed, of the entire Igbo people, patriarchy bowed to womanself.

Efuru would continue to set precedence for other acts and behaviors considered uncharacteristic of women in her society. Unlike other women, Efuru was not unduly worried when it was feared that she might be barren. After a year of marriage, rumors of her possible barrenness started flying but Efuru did not despair. She said to herself: "I am still young, surely, God cannot deny me the joy of motherhood." Even as she reassured herself, she started thinking of getting a second wife for her husband, in case she turned out to be barren! Several times in the novel she had said to people: "It is only a bad woman who wants her husband all to herself." Efuru was so secure in her womanhood and so adjusted to her culture that she thought nothing of sharing her husband. The only thing she would object to was being relegated to the background. She emphasized: "I want to keep my position as the first wife, for it is my right." Efuru was respectful of her culture and so well adjusted that she forced an otherwise anti-woman society to bend backwards to accommodate her special needs.

To be sure that she had covered all the grounds, she and her father went to consult a medicine man about her condition. The diviner recommended a specific sacrifice to Uhamiri the Goddess of the Lake, who wanted Efuru to become her priestess. A couple of months later, Efuru conceived and gave birth to a baby girl. She was fulfilled with her new title of mother. She continued to prosper in her trade and soon became the un-official money-lender of several poor people whose debts she often forgave. She gained the respect and admiration of practically everybody in town.

Unwittingly, Efuru's beauty and prosperity, her popularity and sheer goodness of character frightened and intimidated her husband. He ran away from home under pretext of going on a buying trip. He was away when their only daughter suddenly became ill and died. He was sent for but he never returned. Efuru grieved for her daughter and her husband's desertion. She was never broken even when she found out that her husband was living with another woman. Efuru returned to her father's house after waiting for a reasonable time. When a sympathizer said to her, "I heard you have left your husband," she replied, "No, he has left me." Her sympathizer would whisper to her not to say that. In their culture, a man is not supposed to leave a woman. It is always a woman who leaves a man. But Efuru would retort, "No, he left me." Thus, she let it be known that, though she respected tradition, she rejected practices she found to be unjust to women. Once more her society deferred to Efuru and she got away with utterances and behavior that her people would not tolerate from any other woman.

In addition to being the town's banker, Efuru performed other acts of philanthropy. She sent the father of her maid to the hospital and paid for his surgery and stay. An old woman's money was stolen and Efuru gave her back more than was stolen from her. She rushed to the side of her ex-mother-in-law when she was deathly ill. She sent another old woman to the hospital and paid for her one-month's stay. When the woman's children came to thank her they said to her, "You have done what only men are capable of doing and so you have done like a man. We have no words to thank you." Apparently in her society, acts of benevolence are ascribed to men only!

However, Efuru always forced her way into men's domain and is welcomed and appreciated rather than resented and reprimanded.

When her husband failed to return, Efuru remarried. Her new husband, Gilbert returned the bride price that Efuru's first husband had paid to her father. Her father took the money to his first son-in-law's people and legal divorce took effect. Though Gilbert was a fairly wealthy trader by local standard, he was no match for Efuru in wealth and business acumen. Soon, Efuru convinced him to team up with her in trading. Wealth began to flow and Gilbert built a big house. His mother, who was known to be difficult, fell in love with Efuru and gave her credit for her son's prosperity.

It wasn't long after her marriage to Gilbert that Efuru started getting signs of call to the priesthood of Uhamiri, the goddess of the Lake. Efuru and her father consulted a diviner who confirmed the visions that Efuru had been seeing in her dreams. The diviner listed the ordinance of the deity. She had to build a separate hut for her meetings with the goddess. For those days she had to be pure and avoid contact with her husband. She had to prepare a special dish to share with the deity alone; and she must dress in white for those days. Gilbert helped his wife set up for her priestly position and function. He made sure to observe the rules as they applied to him. Because of Efuru's diligence in worship of her goddess, she experienced greater prosperity and peace than ever before.

The curse of barrenness followed Efuru. This was made worse by the fact that every priestess of Uhamiri suffered childlessness. Therefore, Efuru never got pregnant throughout her marriage to Gilbert. Once more, she took the initiative to get a second wife for Gilbert. Shortly thereafter, Efuru learned that Gilbert had a son out of wedlock with some woman at Ndoni. The second wife was enraged but Efuru was happy for Gilbert. She persuaded Gilbert to bring the little boy to live with them. The little boy was brought home but the second wife made sure he was sent back to his mother. In this instance, Efuru once again demonstrated her self-assurance, her magnanimity and her compliance with those practices she viewed as harmless and worthwhile.

It happened again! Gilbert went on a buying trip but never returned. In his absence, Efuru's father died. He did not return for the funeral. Efuru buried her father, a feat reserved for sons only. When she would not stop weeping, sympathizers reminded her that her father was lucky "because he had a daughter like you to bury him. What if you were not in a position to perform all the ceremonies"? Efuru was thoroughly embarrassed by Gilbert's absence. Yet, when Gilbert returned weeks after the burial, Efuru was relieved to see him alive. Gilbert refused to tell her what happened. It took the town gossip for Efuru to learn that her husband had been in jail. Although going to jail was shameful, what mattered to Efuru was the reason for it. When she confronted Gilbert for an explanation he told her, "I went to jail but I did not steal. I was foolish and I paid for my foolishness." Efuru sighed with relief but asked why he didn't tell her. He replied, "I was afraid that you would be upset. It was fear only, only fear, my wife. Fear that you would desert me." It was unheard of in her culture that a man told his wife that he was afraid of her! But such was the mysterious power of this woman.

Unlike Efuru, who was happy that their husband was not jailed for theft, the younger wife, Nkoyeni had no sympathy for Gilbert when she too, heard through gossip that their husband had been in jail. After fighting with the gossiper at the market place, Nkoyeni came home to fight Gilbert for the truth. Gilbert denied going to jail and Efuru tried to cover up for him. Nkoyeni refused to listen to Efuru who begged her to protect their husband's manhood. She carried on till both Gilbert and Efuru became disgusted with her. Efuru set about arranging for another wife for Gilbert but before the negotiations were finalized, Efuru became critically ill. A meddlesome woman who had been jealous of Efuru, persuaded Efuru's mother-in-law that Efuru would die unless she confessed to committing adultery. In turn, the mother-in-law persuaded her son to ask Efuru to confess to adultery and live. Efuru was too weak to respond but was willing to die than confess to a crime she did not commit.

It took the intervention of Ajanupu, the aunt of her ex-husband, to rescue Efuru from Gilbert's humiliation and harassment. Ajanupu physically fought Gilbert and broke a heavy wooden pestle over his head knocking him unconscious and drawing blood. She then rushed Efuru to the hospital where she fully recovered. When Efuru returned from the hospital, she went back to her father's house. This time she told people unabashedly, "I have left Gilbert." She became more radiant and more prosperous as she continued in her worship of Uhamiri.

At the end of the novel, the author hinted at the mystery and paradox of women's worship of Uhamiri. Why would women who live in a culture that abhorred female infertility, worship a goddess who showed zero tolerance for female fertility? What did women see in this goddess? Could it be her overwhelming beauty, her superfluous wealth? Could it be her contentment and acceptance by men and women, despite her childlessness? Nwapa created Efuru as a metaphor for Uhamiri, a well beloved and highly cherished goddess of a patriarchal society, a society that bows to her orders and her wishes.

In all, Efuru remains the first and perhaps the greatest example of true womanself in African literature. She did not have to fight any of the traditions, yet she succeeded in getting things done her way. By her charisma and the sheer nobility of her character, Efuru received the blessing and cooperation of her society, a patriarchal society.

IRREPRESSIBLE WOMANSELF

Shug Avery and Sofia of *The Color Purple* did not have the captivating beauty and charisma of Efuru. Like Efuru however, they asserted their womanself and forced their society to let them be who they were. Whereas Efuru depended on her stunning beauty, her wealth and her charm to win the respect and acceptance of her society, Shug and Sofia relied on defiance and devil-may-care attitude in their struggle to assert and maintain their womanself.

Before ever Shug appeared on the scene, Celie wrote to God about her illness. The preacher took Shug's illness as text for his sermon. He intoned a catalogue of her sins and the congregation responded "Amen." Shug's notoriety preceded her arrival in town. It seemed like everyone condemned her. Only Albert, Shug's lover of all time, and Celie his wife, sympathized with Shug and came to her rescue. Consequently, Albert or Mr—went to bring Shug to his home, where Celie nursed her back to health. In spite of Shug's frailness, Celie was still smitten by her: "She look so stylish it like the trees all round the house draw themselves up tall for a better look . . .

She look like she ain't long for this world but dressed well for the next."

It didn't matter that Shug was meeting Celie for the first time or that Celie was taking care of her, Shug had to be her nasty cursing self. Yet, her rudeness and apparent ingratitude rendered her more captivating to Celie. Though Shug laughed at Celie and said to her, "You sure is ugly," Celie couldn't help herself muttering: "Lips look like black plum. Eyes big, glossy. Feverish. And mean. Like, sick as she is, if a snake cross her path, she kill it." Shug even barked at Mr—for doting on her: Turn loose my goddam hand. What the matter with you, you crazy? I don't need no little boy . . . hanging on me. I need me a man . . . I don't want to smell no stinking blankety-blank pipe, you hear me, Albert?" Oddly enough, Celie seemed to love and appreciate Shug for her meanness and disrespect for those who obviously cared deeply about her. In fact, Celie felt privileged to minister to Shug as if she were a goddess. She recalled when she gave Shug a bath: I wash her body, it feel like I'm praying. My hands tremble and my breath short . . . I work on her like she a doll . . . I comb and pat, comb and pat."

Shug knew how Celie felt about her. So, finally she said: "Everything I do is fine and dandy to you, Miss Celie. But that's cause you ain't got good sense." This was Shug's speech of acceptance of Celie and the beginning of what would turn into genuine love. Minutes later, Celie sat between Shug and Mr—quilting. Looking at the three of them sitting together, Celie mused, "For the first time in my life, I feel just right."

While Shug was convalescing, Harpo turned a section of his house into a night club. His friend Swain came to pick on his guitar but that wasn't enough to attract clients for three weeks running. Harpo knew that Shug could sing but he was puzzled by her brashness and impolite behavior. He found the courage one day to say to Celie, "Wonder could I get the Queen Honebee? Celie encouraged him to ask her. Shug agreed and Mr—provided Harpo with some old flyers from Shug's trunk. They altered a few things and posted the flyers on trees all over town. The whole town swarmed the place. Celie recalled: "The first Saturday night so many folks come they couldn't get in." Shug's self-styled detractors fumbled for excuses when Shug came down to talk to them. From then on, people could not keep away from Harpo's "Jukejoint." The truth was that people couldn't help admiring Shug for her boldness and devil-may-care attitude toward everything. Mr—was possessive of her and tried to prevent Celie from going to the club. He claimed that wives don't go to places like that, and Shug shot back at him, "Yeah, but Celie going." When Mr—wouldn't stop muttering about the things that he wouldn't allow his wife do, Shug snapped at him, "Good thing I ain't your damn wife," and Mr—hushed right then. And to further damn Mr—, Shug dedicated a song to Celie."

Shug was always on the move and when she told Celie she would be leaving, Celie's heart sank. Shug noticed her saddened feature and wondered why she felt so sad. Celie told her that Mr—would start beating her again if Shug left. Shug reassured her: "I won't leave, until I know Albert won't even think about beating you." Shug had the power to make Mr—do whatever she wanted him to do. To Celie, it was mind boggling that her tyrannical husband would virtually withdraw into himself at the command of Shug. Celie could not fathom this type of power residing in a woman. But she would hear more words and witness acts that would cause her to wonder about the true gender of Shug. For instance, when Sofia came to visit, everyone hugged and made small talk with her. But while Shug was hugging Sofia she said to her, "Girl, you look like a good time, you do." Hearing Shug, Celie commented, "That when I notice how Shug talk and act sometimes like a man. Men say stuff like that to women, Girl, you look like a good time. Women always talk bout hair and health. How many babies living or dead, or got teef." Despite her manly gestures and words, her brashness and impolite behavior, Shug captivated everybody. "All the men got they eyes glued to Shug's bosom. I got my eyes glued there too," Celie said. Why then were men and women drawn to Shug? Could it be because of her irrepressible womanself?

Months after she left Celie and Mr—, Shug returned with Grady whom she introduced as her husband. Shortly after her return, she resumed her lesbian affair with Celie while her new husband and her life-long lover, Mr—, bonded and found amusements for themselves. This time around, Shug told Celie her life history with Mr—. She had three children with Albert but Albert's father wouldn't allow him marry Shug because she supposedly came from trashy background. Albert was forced to marry Annie Julia but Shug continued to sleep with him. She turned Annie's marriage into hell. Now she regretted the misery she caused Annie. Hearing this, Celie felt honored that Shug had asked her, "Do you mind if Albert sleep with me?" To end her story, Shug told Celie how she had left her three children with her mother to pursue a singing career. She enjoyed a bohemian life style, traveling and staying away for months and sometimes, years. When Celie asked if she didn't miss her children she replied, "Naw, I don't miss nothing." Many women would be shocked by Shug's attitude to motherhood. But Shug made no apologies. She didn't have to pretend to be what she was not, and not many women would be bold enough to say they didn't miss their children.

The last surprise that Shug sprang at Celie was when she fell in love with a nineteen-year old boy and decided to go away with him for a fling! Celie was speechless. She could only respond to Shug's questions with scribbles on a piece of paper. Shug went on her knees while tears ran down her face. She begged Celie: "All I ast is six months. Just six months to have my last fling. I got to have it Celie. I'm too weak a woman not to. But if you just give me six months, Celie, I will try to make our life together like it was." What a bisexual animal! Who would have the guts to ask from a lover what Shug just asked Celie? One might call Shug a cradle robber, an immoral or amoral slut, but such labels would not work for Shug. She just had to go after what she desired no matter how other people felt about it. With her disposition to doing whatever she pleased, Shug would carry very well the Igbo name, Mukaosolu—it pleases only me.

Celie and Mr—loved Shug unconditionally. And the majority of their population admired her even if some didn't approve her life style. Shug impressed people because there was no precedent to her behavior and actions. She was passionate and was not afraid or ashamed of her passion. For instance, when she was begging Celie to let her go off with her teenage lover, she said to Celie, "I know how you feel about men. But I don't feel that way. I would never be fool enough to take any of them seriously, but some mens can be a lots of fun." Earlier, Celie had asked if she liked sleeping with Mr—and Shug had replied, "I just love it. Don't you?.

It would take the words of Mr—to capture the essence of Shug's womanself:

"To tell the truth, Shug act more manly than most men. I mean she upright, honest. Speak her mind and the devil take the hindmost. You know Shug will fight . . . She bound to live her life and be herself no matter what."

Sofia, like Shug, lives by her own rules. Again, it is Mr— who best described Sofia and Shug: "Sofie and Shug not like men, but they not like women either. They hold they own, and it's different." Right from childhood, Sofia had to fight to secure a footing in her parents' home. When Celie made the mistake of telling Harpo to beat up Sofia in order to make her obey him, Harpo tried but came home badly beaten up by Sofia. When she confronted Celie for advising Harpo to beat her, she warned Celie by telling her about herself: All my life I had to fight. I had to fight my daddy. I had to fight my brothers. I had to fight my cousins and my uncles. A girl child ain't safe in a family of men." Sofia admitted she loved Harpo and added, But I'll kill him dead before I let him beat me."

Sofia recognized very early, the odds against women in society. She decided to fight and beat those odds no matter under what guise they presented themselves. As a young girl in love, she was not allowed to go out with her boy friend Harpo, because her father felt Harpo was not good enough for her. Sofia responded by carrying on with Harpo in her father's house till she got pregnant. When her father threw her out, Harpo invited her to come and live with him at his father's. Sofia laughed and reminded him that he was still dependent on his father. However she told him, "When you free, me and the baby be waiting." When Harpo got his own place, Sofia married him. Harpo expected Sofia to be a subservient wife like Celie but he soon realized that Sofia was nothing like any woman he knew. Sofia followed her own mind and did as she pleased. In fact, she preferred chores that men traditionally performed. She would rather be out in the fields or fooling with the animals, while Harpo did the dishes. Sofia liked to hunt with bow and arrow. She would climb up the ladder to mend the roof while Harpo watched. She was constantly in physical fights with Harpo because she refused to be a womanbeing. Harpo constantly complained to Celie: "I want her to do what I say, like you do for Pa. She do what she want, don't pay me no mind at all. I try to beat her, she black my eyes."

True to her nature, Sofia got fed up with Harpo's unmanliness and decided to leave. She told Celie, "I'm getting tired of Harpo. All he think about since us married is how to make me mind. He don't want a wife, he want a dog." More over, she's lost sexual interest in him. "I don't like to go to bed with him no more. I used to chase him home from the field. Git all hot just watching him put the children to bed. But no more. Now I feels tired all the time. No interest." Sofia left with her children to live with her sister Odessa. She found a lover there and had a baby with him.

Years later, Sofia came back with six children and a hefty, prizefighter of a man whom she introduced as a friend of the family. One evening when Sofia came to listen to Shug sing at Harpo's nightclub, Harpo's tiny girl friend Squeak, tried to assert her ownership of Harpo. She called Sofia a bitch and told her to leave Harpo alone. Sofia was in no fighting mood and was about to leave. However, the unwary girl had no idea the type of woman Sofia was, so she slapped Sofia across the head. And Celie who was shocked and frightened for the girl commented on what happened next: "Sofia don't even deal in little ladyish things such as slaps. She ball up her fist, draw back, and knock two of Squeak's side teef out. Squeak hit the floor. One toof hanging on her lip, the other one upside in my cold drink glass."

It would take the strong arm of the law to physically restrain Sofia and throw her in jail for twelve years! Why? An innocent wife of the mayor, Miss Millie was so impressed with the way that Sofia's children looked, that she asked Sofia if she would like to become her maid. Sofia who felt insulted replied, "Hell no!" The mayor's wife thought she misheard and asked Sofia what she said. Sofia repeated, "Hell no." The mayor pushed his wife aside and stood before Sofia and asked her, Girl, what you say to Miss Millie?" Sofia replied, "I say, hell no." Once more, not knowing who Sofia was, the mayor slapped her. Sofia knocked the mayor to the ground while her children piled on top of the mayor, doing whatever damage they could till the police came and hauled Sofia off to jail. They beat her almost to death. The policeman thought she must be crazy to do what she did to the mayor. And Mr—tried to protect her from more beating by telling the authorities that madness ran in Sofia's family.

After twelve years, Sofia seemed to have been broken. She told Celie, "Every time they ast me to do something, Miss Celie, I act like I'm you. I jump up and do just what they say . . . I'm a good prisoner. Best convict they ever see. They can't believe I'm the one sass the mayor's wife, knock the mayor down." But the good behavior was just to keep alive. When Celie suggested that she could be released for good behavior, Sofia said:" Good behavior ain't good enough for them. Nothing less than sliding on your belly with your tongue on they boots can even git they attention. I dream of murder, I dream of murder sleep or wake." Sofia's womanself was never subdued and her captors could sense it, especially the mayor's wife who was forever terrified of her. Though she appeared physically weak people were still afraid of her. When Celie hired her to work in her store, she took her no-nonsense attitude with her. The white man who ran the store was scared of her and the day he called her "auntie," Sofia "ast him which colored man his mama sister marry." Her years in prison did not diminish Sofia's stature as a fighter who acted only on her own convictions. Sofia would break with tradition if she felt convinced that she had a better alternative. For instance, when her mother died, Sofia insisted that she and her two sisters would be the pallbearers with their three brothers. Harpo reminded her that only men could be pallbearers. He advised her to act like a woman, that is, to take it easy and cry if she wanted to but not try to take over. She said she could do whatever women did and lift the coffin too. In the end Sofia did as she pleased, she and her sisters along with their brothers carried their mother's coffin into the church and the congregation did not even stir at the unusual sight. "They don't stare at Sofia and her sisters. They act like this the way it always done."

Harpo was never able to figure out why Sofia always did everything her own way. He finally asked her in a very soft voice, "Why you like this, huh? Why you always think you have to do things your own way? I ast your mama bout it one time, while you was in jail." Sofia asked Harpo what her mother told him and he replied, "She say you think your way as good as anybody else's. Plus, it yours." That was it! Sofia believed in herself. She was as good as anybody else. She made no apologies for who she was, what she thought and what she did.

WOMANSELF IN A DEADLY MIX
OF CULTURE AND RELIGION

Ramatoulaye, the heroine of Mariama Ba's award-winning novel, *Long So a Letter*, embodies womanself caught in the web of culture and religion. From her reminiscences in her letter to her friend Aissatou, one could tell that she has held on to her self from the earliest period of her life. Unlike many girls in her time in Africa, Ramatoulaye did not yield to parent-pressure to marry a man that her mother preferred to her other suitors. She followed her heart and married a man of her choice. Because of her preference for the man in the eternal khaki, her willful disobedience and disregard for her mother's feelings, Ramatoulaye went through a dismal marriage ceremony. She recalls:

"Our marriage was celebrated without dowry, without pomp, under the disapproving looks of my father, before the painful indignation of my frustrated mother, under the sarcasm of my surprised sisters, in our town struck dumb with astonishment."

Ramatoulaye was subjected to this public humiliation on her wedding day because she refused to have her self bullied into marrying against her will to please her mother. Unfortunately, her mother would have the last laugh because her forebodings about the marriage and its ultimate break-up would haunt Ramatoulaye for the rest of her life. Contrary to her mother's premonitions, it was neither Modou's sensuality nor his handsomeness that caused him to betray and abandon his wife and their children. It was the combined forces of culture and religion that destroyed Ramatoulaye's marriage and challenged her womanself.

For thirty years, Ramatoulaye and Modou Fall lived a fulfilling and happy married life. We assume they were happy because there was no mention in her long letter of any ill treatment from Modou. They both carried out their assigned duties for the smooth running of their household. We assume that Ramatoulaye was contented because she claimed: "I had never known the sordid side of marriage." From Ramatoulaye's testimony and from the words of her relatives and friends, she did not experience the vicissitudes of wifehood until Modou walked out of their marriage and set up a new family with young Binetou. To find what went wrong in her marriage, Ramatoulaye searched every corner of her memory looking for the crack that could have led to the collapse of her marriage. She found nothing, but was hard put to find a rationale for it:

Was it madness, weakness, irresistible love? What inner confusion led Modou Fall to marry Binetou . . . Madness or weakness? Heartlessness or irresistible love? What inner torment led Modou Fall to marry Binetou?

When Ramatoulaye failed to find any plausible explanation for her husband's perplexing behavior, she blamed it on mid-life crisis. Perhaps, Modou needed some freshness in the marriage or some young blood to inject new life into his aging body. But these were mere conjectures. The real explanation for Modou's action lay in his culture and religion! Both African culture and Islamic religion allow a man to marry more than one wife. Whatever a man's reasons are, he can marry other wives whether or not the first wife approves of his decision. However, he owes his first wife the courtesy of taking her into confidence and politely asking her permission to allow him to marry other women. If polygamy were not sanctioned by African culture and Islamic religion, it is most unlikely that Modou would have just walked out of his marriage and family to marry another woman and start a new family with her. Therefore, Modou's strong allies—his culture and religion—encouraged him to insult and repudiate his wife of thirty years.

Culture and religion created specific conditions for women only. The worst of these harrowing conditions are the rituals of mourning a dead husband. The same rituals are not imposed on husbands when their wives die. Take the case of Ramatoulaye who suddenly became a widow when her husband dropped dead from a heart attack. She recalled and recoiled from the dreaded moment when she would be ritualistically and publicly humiliated. She lamented:

This is the moment dreaded by every Senegalese woman, the moment when she sacrifices her possessions as gifts to her family-in-law; and, worse still, beyond her possessions she gives up her personality, dignity, becoming a thing in the service of the man who has married her (also in the service of the rest of his family members) . . . Her behaviour is conditioned: no sister-in-law will touch the head (to shave it) of any wife who has been stingy, unfaithful or inhospitable.

Ramatoulaye calmly endured the above treatment. Then, for four months and ten days she had to sit on a mat and receive whatever meager service the "guards" of widows would give her. She must make sure to remain unkempt so as to "correctly" mourn for a run-away dead husband. Because she had respect for her culture and religion she complied with their demands:

I hope to carry out my duties fully. My heart concurs with the demands of religion. Reared since childhood on their strict precepts, I expect not to fail. The walls that limit my horizon do not bother me. I have enough memories to ruminate upon.

Indeed, complying with demands meant reminding a woman of her inferior status in her society, it meant reinforcing her state of womanbeing. Yet, for Ramatoulaye, her compliance was an act of faith and of respect for a culture that one could not easily subvert no matter the level of one's western education or exposure to western culture. She was neither forced nor coerced; she just complied.

Now, culture and religion did not demand that Ramatoulaye remain married to Modou after he made a clean break. She could have filed for a divorce. But Ramatoulaye seemed very confused about what action to take. Her own children urged her to leave their father. Daba, her oldest child told her: "Break with him mother! Send this man away. He has respected neither you nor me. Do what Aunty Aissatou did; break with him. Tell me you'll break with him. I can't see you fighting over a man with a girl my age." The decision had to come from Ramatoulaye. Thus, she held long debates with her divided mind. She couldn't figure out how to start again at zero after such a long time living with one man and having twelve children with him. She considered the burden of doing the duties of a mother as well as of a father. She asked herself: "Did I have enough energy to bear alone the weight of this responsibility, which was both moral and material? One mind told her to leave and turn over a new page. Then she listened to the advice of her friends and even of her neighbor, the griot woman. She remembered some abandoned and divorced women she knew, and how they ended up. She thought of her friend Aissatou and of Jacqueline. At last she realized she could draw some lesson from the misfortunes of others. Her situation demanded a strong will. Therefore, she braced her self and looked reality in the face and took a decision:

"Yes, I was well aware of where the right solution lay, the dignified solution. And to my family's great surprise, I chose to remain. Modou and Mawdo were surprised, could not understand . . ."

Ramatoulaye's decision to remain married (in principle) to Modou baffled and angered, not only her children, but also many readers and critics. Many critics see Aissatou as the stronger woman because she did not hesitate to break away from her husband and set the unprecedented example of taking their four sons with her. Ramatoulaye is considered weak for allegedly stepping back into womanbeing. But she did not revert to womanbeing. Her womanself remained intact because she thought and analyzed the entire situation before she made everyone of her choices. She followed her choices with actions, and these are the defining qualities of womanself. That Modou reneged on his duties as a father did not mean that Ramatoulaye should do the same. Instead, she welcomed the challenge of combining the double duties of a mother and a father. She talked of her new life to Aissatou:

I was surviving. In addition to my former duties, I took over Modou's as well . . . The last date for payment of electricity bills and of water rates demanded my attention. I was often the only woman in the queue . . . Replacing the locks and latches of broken doors, replacing broken windows was a bother . . .

In addition to taking on the routine chores of a husband, she now had to run all her errands using public transport. She did not withdraw into herself nor did she stop living. Thus, she grew bolder and started going to social events like the movies unaccompanied by any man: "I survived. I overcame my shyness at going alone to cinemas; I would take a seat with less and less embarrassment as the months went by."

More important than single handedly taking care of her family was her insightful apprehension of the implications of her leaving the marriage. If she left, then, Modou would have won twice! She and Modou had worked hard for their possessions that included their house and bank account. Already, Modou had mortgaged their home to buy a villa he shared with Binetou. Therefore, Ramatoulaye was entitled to what was left of their common property. Why should she leave it for Modou to do as he pleased? In fact, events proved her decision to be right when Modou stopped coming to the house. She told Aissatou:

I survived. The more I thought about it, the more grateful I became to Modou for having cut off all contact. I had the solution my children wanted-the break without having taken the initiative . . . I faced up to the situation bravely. I carried out my duties; they filled the time and channeled my thoughts.

Ramatoulaye resolved to push despair away and get on with the life of a single mother even as she remained married in name to Modou. When everyone realized that her mind was made up, they began to say that she had been bewitched. Then there were countless suggestions of how to dislodge the spell of witchcraft. Many recommended the services of a marabout or those of powerful medicine men from neighboring Mali. But Ramatoulaye held on to her convictions. She reasoned:

To act as I was urged would have been to call myself into question . . . Was I to deny myself because Modou had chosen another path? No, I would not give in to pressure. My mind and my faith rejected supernatural power. They rejected this easy attraction, which kills any will to fight. I looked reality in the face.

She was not embarrassed to recognize that Binetou and her mother constituted the reality; they lured her husband away. She recognized the combined weight of culture and religion that allowed men to do as they pleased with women. She decided to deal with the immediate reality the best way she knew how. She staked her claim and remained where she was, until death intervened to remove Modou from the scene. How else could Ramatoulaye have demonstrated her womanself? She was a separate person from her husband; she had a mind and a will of her own. She was not going to step on live coal because Modou did so!

Despite the failure of her marriage, Ramatoualye did not denounce the marriage institution. She unabashedly declared, "I am one of those who can realize themselves fully and bloom only when they form part of a couple . . . even though I respect the choice of liberated women, I have never conceived of happiness outside of marriage." With this shocking avowal, one would expect her to jump at the next offer, nay, at two offers of marriage. First, she humiliated her brother-in-law with her bold and crushing words of rejection, in front of his two witnesses. She addressed Tamsir:

You forget that I have a heart, a mind; that I am not an object to be passed from hand to hand. You don't know what marriage means to me: it is an act of faith and of love, the total surrender of oneself to the person one has chosen and who has chosen you.

What of your wives Tamsir? . . . I shall never be the one to complete your collection. My house shall never be for you the coveted oasis . . . abundance and calm! No, Tamsir! Purge yourself of your dreams of conquest . . . I shall never be your wife.

Secondly, she turned down the offer of Dr. Daouda Dieng, a long time admirer whom her mother had wanted her to marry. In her rejection of Dr. Dieng, Ramatoulaye demonstrated the nobility of her character. She was aware of the advantages of marrying this wealthy man with an impeccable reputation for goodness. But she refused this offer because, "My heart does not love Daouda Dieng. My mind appreciates the man. But my heart and mind often disagree." But, the more important reason is the one she gives in her letter of rejection to him:

My conscience is not accommodating enough to enable me to marry you . . . Esteem is not enough for marriage, whose snares I know from experience. And then the existence of your wife and children further complicates the situation. Abandoned yesterday because of a woman, I cannot lightly bring myself between you and your family.

Only a woman secure in her self could have refused such a tempting offer that would have brought her more comfort and even more love than she received from Modou. Besides, only a woman of noble character would pass off such an opportunity to cause pain to another because she had suffered pain at the hands of a fellow woman. Ramatoulaye's refusal of two marriage offers spoke to her self pride and self assurance. It certainly spoke to her womanself.

Furthermore, the way Ramatoulaye handled various problems of parenting showed that she was a woman in control. She never allowed popular opinion or practice to dictate her responses to situations. For instance, when she found out that her daughter Aissatou was pregnant, she did not go insane with rage. Instead, she pondered the role of a mother when her children make mistakes. She understood her daughter's predicament and offered comfort. Then, she worked with her daughter and her future son-in-law to solve the problem. Needless to say, she shocked her griot neighbor and others who expected her to punish her daughter in some way. However, she handled the situation in a way that promoted ideal parenting with unconditional love for the offspring.

Considering the ways that Ramatoulaye dealt with all the problems that confronted her from the break up of her marriage to the aftermath of Modou's death, one could not impute any type of weakness to her character. It was in deference to culture and religion that she subjected herself to ritual mourning for her deserting husband. She was not forced to stay married to Modou. She chose to stay because she chose the man she married. Besides, her marriage vow meant a great deal to her, and that is a point of strength and not of weakness. On the whole, Ramatoulaye never gave womanbeing a chance to surplant her womanself.

Aissatou, the great friend and confidant of Ramatoulaye, was equally caught in the deadly mix of culture and religion. She and Mawdo had loved and chosen each other. They married against the wishes of Mawdo's mother who felt that her son had married beneath his aristocratic origin. Mawdo's mother claimed that her son's royal blood had been contaminated by Aissatou, the goldsmith's daughter. She vowed to get even with the upstart. While her son and his wife settled in their marriage, and had four sons, she groomed the instrument of her revenge-her niece, Nabou. And while the entire town knew of her mother-in-law's plot to bring in a second wife for Mawdo, Aissatou was in the dark and happy in her marriage.

After Nabou had been raised to become a docile wife and trained as a midwife, her aunt literally thrust her upon her cousin Mawdo. Mawdo's mother told him: "I will never get over it if you don't take her as your wife. Shame kills faster than disease." Again, the same culture and religion that allowed a man to marry many wives prevailed. Mawdo dared not disobey his mother. Nabou became his wife! Even though Mawdo still loved Aissatou, he could not bring himself to talk or reason with her. He hoped she would stay in the marriage.

Unlike Ramatoulaye, Aissatou's response was swift. She paid no attention to the advice of her well-wishers. She would never negotiate her status in their marriage and she would not consider sharing her husband with another woman. She was defiant of cultural and religious demands. Therefore, Aissatou chose to make a clean break. She took her four sons and left Mawdo.

In her scathing parting letter to Mawdo, one could discern an iron-willed woman of uncompromising principles. After examining the societal ordering of human affairs and destinies that every one seemed to buy into, Aissatou told Mawdo:

"I will not yield to it. I cannot accept what you are offering me in place of the happiness we once had. You want to draw a line between heartfelt love and physical love . . . If you can procreate without loving, merely to satisfy the pride of your declining mother, then I find you despicable . . . I am stripping myself of your love, your name. Clothed in my dignity, the only worthy garment, I go my way . . . Goodbye.

Aissatou was not afraid to start again from zero; she took her life and the lives of her four sons into her hands. She went back to school and studied Translation. She graduated and secured a job as an interpreter in the Senegalese Embassy in the United States. She made enough money for her family and had more to buy a new car for her friend Ramatoulaye! Instead of suffering from her husband's betrayal, it was her husband who suffered from her leaving. He constantly asked Ramatoulaye about her friend and Ramatoulaye reported to Aissatou: "Your departure had truly shaken him. His sadness was clearly evident. When he spoke of you, the inflexions in his voice hardened."

Although many critics think that Aissatou is the stronger of the two women, and they prefer her clear-cut way of handling a similar situation, others, including this author believe that Ramatoulaye is an equally strong character. She might take a longer and tortuous approach to her problems, she nonetheless arrived at solutions that preserved her dignity and did honor to her womanhood. Still, some might look at the two friends as two sides of the same coin.

Fusena, another Muslim educated girl in Ama Ata Aidoo's *Changes*, is another good example of womanself caught in a deadly mix of culture and religion. Like Ramatoulaye and Aissatou, Fusena attended a teacher training college. It was at that college that she met Ali, who was one of her classmates. They became close, not as lovers but as friends. By the time they graduated, their relationship could be described as platonic on the surface. Deep down, they felt differently but they held down their emotions. At the end of their training, they were posted to different schools in the same area, so they continued to be "good friends" and to relate as such.

At twenty-six, Fusena was still unmarried. She had refused many offers of marriage but her mother was hoping she would accept a rich Alhaji who was seriously courting her. As she continued to show no interest, the Alhaji suspected that Ali might be the reason. He sent his thugs to warn Ali who denied any romantic involvement with Fusena. Ali further claimed that Fusena was like a sister to him. He promised to help the Alhaji win Fusena's hand.

In their third year of teaching at Tamale, Ali was awarded a scholarship for degree studies in Britain. A bachelor at twenty-eight, Ali would be vulnerable and an easy target for women in Britain. Therefore, Ali went to Fusena and asked her to marry him. She was surprised but she accepted his proposal. Ali went home to announce to his family, the good news of his scholarship and marriage proposal to Fusena. Within a couple of months, marriage negotiations were concluded and Fusena and Ali were legally married in the Muslim tradition. It was decided that Fusena should continue teaching while Ali went over to England, settle down and send for Fusena. One thing both families insisted on was that Ali should make sure that Fusena was pregnant before he left the country. Of course, nobody ever thinks of asking an African woman when or if she wanted to start having children right after her wedding. After all, having children is the purpose of marriage to begin with.

Three years later, Ali sent for Fusena and their son Adam. Like many other African wives before her, Fusena looked forward to joining her husband and to doing something on her own to improve herself. By the time she arrived in London, Ali had obtained his first degree and had a full time job. He was also studying part-time for his Master's in Business Administration. Fusena on the other hand sat at home in their one bedroom apartment or did her housework and looked through catalogues. Soon after, she became pregnant with their second child. When the baby came, she nursed it, looked after Adam and Ali, kept house and stared at London's bleak and wet views.

Then, she suddenly awakened to her situation! She had become a housewife who must behave and act as her husband demanded. It dawned on her that she had lost her self and the freedom to choose what she wanted to do with her life. Where was the original Fusena who interacted on equal footing with Ali before their marriage? She finally admitted to herself that by marrying Ali, she had exchanged a friend for a husband. The first time this hit her, she actually sat down and wept bitterly. She also knew immediately that there was nothing she could do about her situation.

Fusena felt trapped in what she saw as a helpless situation. She considered it impossible and even useless to leave Ali. She reasoned that Ali the husband would never revert to Ali the friend if she divorced him. She would only have an estranged husband. Most importantly, she kept telling herself that given the position of women in society, she would rather be married than not, and rather to Ali than anyone else. Such was the power of a culture that had no room for single and independent women. This culture continues to push the belief: nma nwanyi wu di-the beauty of a woman is a husband. Fusena found it futile to assert her self in a culture that enslaved her through marriage. On the other hand, one would have expected Ali, the educated and westernized African to maintain an equal partnership in marriage with his former classmate and friend. But, Ali was a product of the same culture that treated a woman as an appendage to a man at best.

Another set back for Fusena was watching Ali get more and more educated while she did not. Although she felt miserable about it, she dared not raise the issue with Ali who was practically getting ready for the journey back home. On reaching home, Fusena discovered she was pregnant with their third child. Once more she was busy nursing and helping Ali find a place for them to live. She started keeping house again. All along, she longed to go back to teaching. But, after two years of trying to settle down, she could not even remember how it felt to be in a classroom. She knew it would be difficult to pick up from where she left in her teaching profession. However, her problem was compounded by Ali's lack of support for her. He told her: "It is a waste of time. The hours are long and the pay is terrible. There should be a more lucrative job you could do and still have time to look after the children." For Fusena however, it was not a question of something lucrative with abundant time to spare. It was the question of doing what she wanted and loved to do. In fact, it was the principle of it all, of choosing and doing what gave her the greatest satisfaction. Again, culture prevailed; Ali had the final word. Consequently, he bought her a massive kiosk at a strategic site in Accra. Within a short time people started talking about Fusena's kiosk: They were saying she made more money from the kiosk than the largest supermarket in town. Fusena was not impressed; she only smiled to herself because she derived no satisfaction from her lucrative business.

As if she didn't have enough to aggravate her, Ali came home to tell her that he was planning to marry Esi, a woman he had been seeing for quite some time. He had not thought it necessary to discuss his plans for a second wife with Fusena. When he told Esi that he wanted to marry her, she asked: "And your wife?" Ali was surprised by the question and he asked Esi, "Where does she (Fusena) come in?" Esi replied:

"Everywhere . . . What does she feel about it? Or you have not discussed your plans for me with her?" Ali lied by saying that he had talked to Fusena; he tried to convince Esi not to worry about the feelings of Fusena. Here again, one sees how culture and religion empower men to disregard the very humanity of women, not to talk of their feelings. Ali knew that Fusena was not going to "raise hell" about his running around with other women or his plans to get a second wife. Ali knew that Fusena inevitably guessed when he was having a serious affair with another woman. There was an unspoken agreement between them not to talk about these affairs, that was all. He convinced himself that he did not operate on a level of excesses that would leave his wife's feelings unnecessarily bruised. After all, he loved his wife and he tried not to hurt her deliberately!

On Fusena's part, she was not really angered by Ali's love affairs because adultery was a man's prerogative in her culture. She was not surprised that Ali was getting a second wife because she was raised to accept polygamy. What bothered her was the fact that the second wife had a university degree and she, the first wife did not! She felt deeply humiliated. She felt the injustice of not being allowed to further her education when she had the opportunity to do so. Thus, when Ali told her that he was thinking of marrying another wife, Fusena asked, "She has a university degree?" Ali was taken aback by Fusena's unexpected response, so he too asked, "What has that got to do with it?" "Everything," she shot back. Fusena could no longer contain her anguish. She drove out recklessly to let off some steam and to seek counseling from the elders in their family. The older women calmed her down and reminded her of her privileged position as the first wife. Fusena was not comforted by her privileged position in the marriage.

Once more, culture blocked Fusena's path to action. Rebelling was not an option, so she had to go along with Ali's desires. Ali married Esi, an independent woman who lived in her own house in another section of the town. Throughout the course of the story, the two co-wives never met. There was no remarkable change in the timetable and routine of Fusena and Ali's marriage. On the other hand, the second wife received a rougher deal because she saw less of Ali after their marriage than she did when they were courting. Ali merely popped in from his travels to load her with presents and snatch a few hours of intimacy and loving. In the third year of their marriage Esi could not cope any more. She broke up with Ali but did not file for a divorce. She remained friends with Ali and continued to be his wife in name only.

So, why did Ali marry a second wife? He did, because his culture said he could.

With the backing of his culture, Ali couldn't care less what anxiety and heartache he caused the two women. After all, in his culture, a man always gained in stature through any way he chose to associate with a woman. And that included adultery. On the other hand, a woman is always diminished in her association with a man. And why did Fusena and Esi remain married to Ali? They did, because their culture decreed that the beauty of a woman is a husband, no matter how cruel and ugly the man. Every wife had to allow her self to be swallowed or destroyed through marriage. Aidoo phrased it best when she said: "A good woman was she who quickened the pace of her own destruction. To refuse as a woman to be destroyed, was a crime that society spotted very quickly and punished swiftly and severely."

A normal marriage in Africa presupposes the death of womanself and the ascendancy of womanbeing. Thus, Aidoo compares the fate of a bride on her wedding day to the fate of a death row inmate on the eve of his execution. Both are granted their wishes because their death was imminent. The bride was made much of, because that whole ceremony was a funeral of the self that could have been. Fusena was first silenced and then swallowed by marriage. She lacked the strength and resolve of Ramatoulaye and Aissatou who fought their culture and won even as each of them retained her womanself.

SUSPENDED WOMANSELF: TAMBUDZAI

Tambudzai, the narrator and major character in *Nervous Conditions* is a good example of suspended self. From very early in her life, Tambudzai's vibrant self asserted itself. As early as eight years old, this little girl questioned and challenged the gender bias that favored males over females in her family. She had observed that "the needs and sensibilities of the women in my family were not considered a priority, or even legitimate." It was for that reason that she was two years behind where she should have been in school at her age. She felt this injustice so keenly that she came to dislike her brother especially and her parents for their undisguised favoritism for her brother. Her anger reached its peak when her father decided to withdraw her from school because they could not afford the fees for her though they could for her brother. Her father argued that sending girls to school was a waste of money because girls do get married. Tambu reminded him that Maiguru, her uncle's wife was educated. When she saw that her father would not be persuaded, she turned to her mother for support but what she received was a "lecture" on the burden of womanhood. Furthermore, her mother began to prepare her for disappointment by discouraging her. When she realized that her mother took her father's side, she turned to her brother for solidarity, but he too was against her going to school.

Tambu boldly confronted her father with a proposition that would have made any parent proud. She said to her father: "I will earn the fees. If you will give me some seed, I will clear my own field and grow my own maize. Not much. Just enough for the fees. Her father laughed derisively in her face and ridiculed her: "Just enough for the fees! Can you see her there? Such a little shrub, but already making ripe plans!" He turned to his wife and asked her to tell her daughter that there was no money. Her mother who seemingly took her side this time asked her husband: And did she ask for money? Listen to your child. She is asking for seed. That we can give her. Let her try. Let her see for herself that some things cannot be done. We see that her mother's support was not genuine. She was convinced that her daughter would fail, therefore, the least they could do was to give her a chance to fail. Though she knew her daughter's determination, she still underestimated her knowledge and skill in market gardening, a skill she mastered very early by watching and working with her grandmother.

Tambu received a piece of land; she cleared it and planted maize seeds. She tended her plot as a mother her newborn. She watched her maize grow and bear fruits. She watched them more closely while she waited for them to ripen. As she waited to harvest her crop, she doubted that she would raise enough money for her fees: "I had to be careful in thinking about the harvest in case I was discouraged. I had to push away the knowledge that I could not earn much from my crop."

As soon as the crops were ripe, they began to disappear. When she complained to her brother, he taunted her: "What did you expect? Did you really think you could send yourself to school?" She received no support from anyone in her family, yet she remained confident and undaunted and even decided to take a break and go to church. It was at Sunday school that she learned that her brother had been stealing her mealies and sharing them with other children. She charged at her brother at the football field. Narrating the incident she said:

"I remember at one moment playing pada, the next Nhamo and I rolling about in the dirt of the football pitch, a group of excited peers egging us on. They said I went straight for my brother and brought him down in a single charge. The element of surprise was on my side. I sat on top of him, banged his head into the ground, screamed and spat and cursed. Nhamo heaved. I fell off him . . ."

It took the intervention of the Sunday school teacher, Mr. Matimba to break up the fight. Such were the strength and the determination of this young child to fend for herself in a world where the odds were against females. When Mr. Matimba heard the story of her little gardening and the reason for the fight, he was sympathetic. For the first time an adult listened to Tambudzai and understood her need. Mr. Matimba offered to take her to town where she would make more money selling her green maize. When she told her father about Matimba's suggestion, he again laughed in her face and ordered his wife to "tell this child of yours she cannot go to town with that man." Once more, her mother pretending to be on her side asked her husband:

"And why should I tell her such things? The girl must have a chance to do something for herself, to fail for herself . . . You know your daughter. She is willful and headstrong. She won't listen to me . . . She must see these things for herself. If you forbid her to go, she will always think you prevented her from helping herself. She will never forget it, never forgive you."

Tambu went with Mr. Matimba to sell her maize in town. As her fate would have it, a benevolent white lady-Doris, saw her inviting people to buy her maize. Doris was outraged. She proceeded to give Matimba a piece of her mind: "Child labour. Slavery! That's what it is . . . The child ought to be in school learning her tables and keeping out of mischief . . ." Finally, when Mr. Matimba got the chance to defend himself, he spoke most sorrowfully and most beseechingly. Doris darkened like a chameleon. Money changed hands, paper money from Doris' hands to Mr. Matimba's. Doris donated ten pounds towards Tambu's school fees. Mr. Matimba arranged to deposit the money with the headmaster who would apply the money to Tambu's fees till it ran out.

Tambu went home and told her parents what happened; her father didn't believe her story. He went to the headmaster and he confirmed the story and showed him the receipt made out to his daughter. He demanded the money because his daughter's money was his. Mr. Matimba tried to explain to him that Tambu would make more than ten pounds a month when she finished school. Jeremiah, Tambu's father, was scandalized and he asked Mr. Matimba, "Have you ever heard of a woman who remains in her father's house? She will meet a young man and I will have lost everything."

In the end, Tambu triumphed and went back to school and proved her worth by taking the first position in her classes for two consecutive years. Her family members were not impressed. They said she repeated a class in the first instance and she was older the next time, so they explained away her brilliant performance. She was in school when her uncle and his family returned from England and took her brother to live at the mission with them. Unfortunately her brother died not too long after he moved to the mission. Babamukuru's plan to elevate Jeremiah's family by educating his son Nhamo, came to an abrupt end. Jeremiah had no other male child to take Nhamo's place at the mission. That was how Babamukuru broke the rules by taking Tambudzai, a girl, to take her brother's place at the mission; to be the one to pull her family out of poverty.

The foregoing is the history of young Tambudzai before she left her home in the village to live with her uncle Babamukuru and his family at the mission. Before her move to the mission, Tambu was a fearless self-assured child who questioned things. She literally challenged the traditional practice of favoring boys over girls; she won her battle to be given a chance to prove that she could take care of her needs. Thus, at the age of eight, Tambu asked for a piece of land and seed to raise her own crops and pay her school fees! She succeeded beyond her expectations.

Tambu's transformation began when she went to live at the mission. She referred to her move as her reincarnation. Reincarnation is an appropriate description because Tambu's old self died, and a new young girl emerged, trapped between a self and a being. Faced with the dreadful choice between self-assertion and pure survival Tambu chose the latter. She could not forget the reason for her transfer to the mission:

"Consciously I thought my direction was clear. I was being educated. When I had been educated, I would find a job and settle down to it, carrying on, in the time that was available before I was married into a new home, Babmukuru's great work of developing the family."

To achieve the above goal, Tambu decided to put a lid on her self. She accepted her status of a poor relation who must do whatever was necessary to "merit" and maintain the charity she was to receive from her uncle. The first rule for survival and therefore achieving her goal was to be submissive:

"I had grown much quieter and more self effacing than was usual, even for me. Beside Nyasha I was a paragon of feminine decorum, principally because I hardly ever talked unless spoken to . . . Above all, I did not question things. It did not matter to me why things should be done this way rather than that way. I simply accepted that this was so . . . As a result of all these things that I did not think or do, Babamukuru thought I was the sort of young woman a daughter ought to be . . ."

Tambu put on the cloak of womanbeing to achieve her goal of lifting her family out of poverty. She no longer questioned things, even things she knew to be wrong or ridiculous. For instance, she strongly resented her uncle's decision to force her parents into having a church wedding after nineteen years of marriage:

"The whole business reduced my parents to the level of the stars of a comic show. I did not want to see them brought down like that and I certainly did not want to be a part of it. I couldn't simply go up to Babamukuru and tell him what I thought . . . So, I pretended to myself that the wedding was a wonderful plan, just what my parents needed."

The once vocal and confrontational child lost her earlier nerves. She became vague in her thinking and confused in her responses, all because of her uncle's over powering personality. She laments: "My vagueness and my reverence for my uncle, what he was, what he had achieved, what he represented and therefore what he wanted, had stunted the growth of my faculty of criticism, sapped the energy that in childhood I had used to define my own position." She nostalgically recalls how she used to stand up to her father. Now she is unable to tell her uncle that his wedding was a farce. She chose to suffer in silence and her pent-up emotions affected her physical being. For, on the morning of the wedding she could not get up from the bed. She became temporarily paralyzed; no amount of threatening from her uncle could force her muscles to respond. It no longer mattered whether she was sent home packing or not. Her uncle did not know how much she suffered internally over the question of that wedding. No one knew how her mind had raced and spun and ended up splitting into two disconnected entities that had long frightening arguments with each other . . .

Tambu disobeyed her uncle. She did not attend the wedding. She prepared herself for the repercussions. Sure enough, she received fifteen lashes of the cane plus two weeks of housework. Tambu stoically went ahead with the punishment. She knew she had to do this to achieve that primary goal of survival. She was willing to do whatever it took to increase her chances to better her lot in life and that of her entire family. It was for this reason that she saw her admission to a Catholic convent as the final step to her freedom:

Going to the convent was a chance to lighten those burdens by entering a world where burdens were light. I would take the chance. I would lighten my burdens. I would go. If Babamukuru would let me. And that was not all. Education at the convent would yield far more positive results than broadening her mental horizon: It meant another step away from the flies, the smells, the fields and the rags, from empty stomachs, from dirt and disease; from my father's abject obeisance to Babamukuru and my mother's chronic lethargy . . w. She was not going to ruin this chance by questioning things. She weighed the prospect and the price of this freedom and decided that the cost would balance.

Furthermore, Tambu had learned that a Catholic institution posed an enormous challenge to young people, especially those raised in Protestant homes. However, she was discerning enough to state:

What I needed I would take with me, the rest I would discard. It would be worth it to dress my sisters in pretty clothes, feed my mother until she was plump and energetic again, stop my father making a fool of himself every time he came into Babamukuru's presence. Money would do all this for me. With the ticket I would acquire attending the convent I would earn lots of it.

Tambu was allowed to go to the convent. She applied herself seriously to her studies. It took no time for the knowledge she gained at the convent to start nudging at her hibernating self. By the time of her graduation she was able to put things into proper perspective with regard to the place of Sacred Heart in her life. In the end, she realized:

"I could no longer accept Sacred Heart and what it represented as a sunrise on my horizon. Quietly, unobtrusively and extremely fitfully, something in my mind began to assert itself, to question things and refuse to be brainwashed, bringing me to this time when I can set down this story."

Like some other female characters before her, Tambudzai's womanself had to be suspended for a period of time. Unlike them however, her situation was different. For instance, Amaka and Janie were much older married women who had the option to walk away from marriage or to stay and fight to the finish. Amaka walked away to make her fortune and Janie fought and waited it out to inherit Joe. But Tambu was a mere child whose very survival depended on the generosity of her deified uncle. Her transfer from her parents' home and supervision to her uncle's was a veritable mission she needed to accomplish to liberate herself and her immediate family from poverty. She would not risk a brighter future for the sake of self-assertion. She needed to get herself well grounded and positioned to take charge of her life and then take care of her family. Tambu didn't have the choice that the older women had. Yet, her age notwithstanding, she made a wise choice to suspend her self. Unlike her aunt Maiguru, she had no investments-husband and children—to pull her back to womanbeing. She knew that her self would eventually reclaim and actualize itself.

A HYPER WOMANSELF: NYASHA

Nyasha and her brother Chido were whisked away to England by their parents-Babamukuru and Maiguru—who had gone there for further studies. Living in England would mean better living condition and superior education. However, the effects of this early uprooting would be disastrous for the children upon their return to Africa, especially for Nyasha.

To begin with, the children had become "too anglicised. They picked up all these disrespectful ways in England, and it's taking them time to learn how to behave at home again." Nyasha was the worse afflicted with assimilation; she became a source of embarrassment for her parents and their relatives. She was unpredictable in her responses to situations, so her relatives were always on the edge of their seats around Nyasha. At any time and without second thoughts she could say or do what her people considered unAfrican or unfeminine. Besides, Nyasha's personality with her irreverent glamorous ways alienated her from her school mates. It frightened and intimidated her cousin Tambudzai who thought that sharing a room with Nyasha would be bad for her. Tambu analyzed

Nyasha thus: Everything about her spoke of alternatives and possibilities that if considered too deeply would wreak havoc with the neat plan I had laid out for my life." Thus, her parents now have this new burden of re-educating Nyasha in African ways. To this effect, her mother apologetically said:

"We keep trying to teach her the right manners, always telling Nyasha, do this; Nyasha, why didn't you do that. But it's taking time. Her head is full of loose connections that are always sparking . . . That child of mine has her own thoughts about everything."

It appears the parents under-estimated the havoc done to the children's sensibility when they were torn away from their original culture while still in their pre-adolescent years. At that impressionable age the children quickly absorbed the new culture and lived within it for five years. Returning to Africa at the onset of adolescence, things came to a head. They experienced genuine culture shock on re-entering the village. Nyasha talked candidly to Tambu about the experience they had on their first day in the village:

"Actually we were frightened that day. And confused. You know, it's easy to forget things when you're that young. We had forgotten what home was like. I mean really forgotten-what it looked like, what it smelt like, all the things to do and say and not to do and say. It was all strange and new. Not like anything we were used to. It was a real shock!"

Considering the hassle and frustrations attendant upon retraining the children, Nyasha felt it was a mistake on their parents' part to have removed them from home:

We shouldn't have gone. The parents ought to have packed us off home . . . May be that would have been best. For them at least, because now they're stuck with hybrids for children.

And they don't like it. I can't help having been there and grown into the me that has been there. But it offends them. I offend them. Really, it's very difficult.

For her part, Nyasha has too many odds stacked against her. She is trapped in the wheels of assimilation. She is victimized by her femaleness. She has the heavy heels of patriarchy resting upon her self-awareness.

The narrator described Nyasha with a string of loaded adjectives-far-minded, isolated, rambunctious and rebellious. To top it off, the word daughter is superimposed on these adjectives, each of which would have a direct impact on the outcome of her fate. At fifteen, Nyasha is far-minded. By this we mean that her intellectual apprehension of her world is light years ahead of her age. It stretches far beyond the limit allowed her gender. When placed side by side with her father, Nyasha's perception of their world dwarfs her father's. Nyasha's worldly wisdom would pose the second great danger to her womanself because women are not expected to be smart, let alone smarter than men, worse still, smarter than their fathers!

Nyasha's analytic mind delved beyond the obvious paternalism of her father and his colonial fathers. She could read the motives and guilt-driven gestures of kindness and generosity displayed by her father and his colonial counterparts. Unfortunately for Nyasha, her accurate readings of her father's motives and actions were not lost on the highly regarded patriarch. In fact, Nyasha's awareness of the inner workings of her father's mind was like the proverbial case of "a child seeing his father's nakedness" and such a sight never failed to blind the child.

The narrator intimated that Nyasha had on numerous occasions disrespected and trampled on her father's position as a man, as head of family, as leader of community and above all as father. Which man would tolerate insults by anyone let alone his own daughter? Therefore, we are not surprised to watch Babamukuru in a fistfight, rolling on the floor with his daughter. Babamuku's honor was at stake and he sought satisfaction from a formidable opponent. He was ready to kill Nyasha and hang himself because,

She has dared to raise her fist against me. She has dared to challenge me. Me! Her father. I am telling you, today she will not live. We cannot have two men in this house. Not even Chido, you hear that Nyasha? Not even your brother there dares to challenge my authority . . . Your salvation lies in going away from my house. For ever. Otherwise, I-will-kill-you.

It was bad enough for a daughter to present herself as a person intellectually aware of things that are given to men only to know. But it was unpardonable for a daughter to challenge her father with her knowledge. Babamukuru would have been more tolerant and more forgiving if the scrutiny and criticism of his actions had come from his son. Thinking of the benign incident that escalated into a physical fight, the narrator felt that Babamukuru was making his daughter a victim of her femaleness.

Later when Chido went to get Nyasha to come into the house, he pleaded with Nyasha to stop upsetting their mother with her reckless behavior: "Don't upset her any more," he told her. "She doesn't need it." "What about me?" Nyasha asked plaintively. "Does anyone care what I need?" Chido answered, "You are the daughter, there are some things you must never do." Nyasha is trapped in her position as daughter and victimized by her gender. She is also victimized by her keen awareness of the inner functioning of her society. In effect, Nyasha has stolen fire from the gods but has not shared it with the rest of her kind.

Nyasha has become too mentally aware for her father's comfort and for her own sanity. She has become intellectually aware of many areas such as History, Politics, Economics, Education and social status. Ironically, being this aware was dangerous for Nyasha because she was only a daughter! And such awareness was the preserve of men. Such multifaceted mental awareness would have been encouraged and admired in her brother. For her sin therefore, Babamukuru will kill Nyasha or have her banished from his family. Eventually Nyasha would serve her punishment and Babamukuru would be satisfied?

Everyone considered Nyasha rebellious. Yet, by her British upbringing, she was just being herself; she was reacting like any normal teenager of same background. As her mother put it, "Her head is full of loose connections that are always sparking. Nyasha has her own thoughts about everything." And in her own words, Nyasha called herself a hybrid. She belonged neither here nor there and her reactions were unique to her. She had not the cultural inhibitions of children raised in the village. Therefore, she would talk back to her parents and question the rationale for the rules they laid down for their children.

For instance, when her mother said she should not read novels by D. H. Lawrence, she wanted to know why it was inappropriate for her. Her mother had no answer except that decent girls shouldn't read such books. "It's only a book and I'm only reading it" she said. A regular African child would not pursue the matter in that tone.

When Babamukuru came to the table and his wife showed him the novel that Nyasha was reading he was distressed, hurt and annoyed. "I don't know what's wrong with our daughter. She has no sense of decency, none whatsoever," he commented. Then he took the book away and returned to the table. When Nyasha came back from the kitchen and discovered the book missing, she wondered what happened to it. She didn't think that her mother would take away the book without her permission. When she started inquiring, her mother said, "Sit down, Nyasha. For God's sake don't carry on about that book. I told you I don't want you reading books like that." Nyasha was unbelieving! "You haven't taken it, have you? She asked. Then followed this exchange:

"Sorry mum. I know you wouldn't do anything like that."

"And what if I have?"

"But you wouldn't, would you? Not without telling me, would you? But Mum! How could you? Without even telling me. That's-that's—I mean, you shouldn't-you have no right to-" At this point, her father couldn't take it any more, so he intervened:

"Er, Nyasha, I don't want to hear you talk to your mother like that"

"But, Dad, I'd expect, really, I'd expect-"

"I expect you to do as I say. Now sit down and eat your food."

"Excuse me."

"Now where are you going? Didn't you hear me tell you I don't want to hear you answer me back? Now sit down and eat that food. All of it. I want to see you eat all of it."

"I've had enough. Really, I'm full."

Nyasha left the dining room and went to the back yard to smoke a cigarette! To her cousin Tambu and to any other African, Nyasha was reckless in her behavior towards her parents. But to Nyasha and her English mentality, she was in the right. Nobody, not even her parents had the right to dictate what she should read! Besides, her educated parents should know something about academic freedom! But her parents are Africans and no amount of British education could erase that truth! No African child says to her parents, "you have no right to interfere in my affairs." Such an utterance is taboo, and an unpardonable affront to a parent.

The worst rebellious act by Nyasha was the one that led to the physical fight between her and her father. Once more, instead of keeping quiet, Nyasha insisted on answering and talking back. Her brother was infuriated by Nyasha's obstinacy and he blurted out: "The little fool, why does she always have to stand up to him?" But Nyasha continued to argue with her father:

"What do you want me to say? You want me to admit I'm guilty, don't you? All right then. I was doing it, whatever you're talking about. There. I've confessed."

Don't talk to me like that, child. You must respect me. I am your father. And in that capacity I am telling you, I-am-telling-you, that I do not like the way you are always walking about with these young men . . . What's the matter with you, girl? Why can't you behave like a young woman from a decent home?

Instead of letting the matter rest, Nyasha continued to defend her actions until her father finally snapped and dealt a heavy blow to her face. He continued hitting her while Nyasha continued telling him to stop hitting her. As he wouldn't stop, Nyasha punched him in the eye and hell broke loose. Babamukuru bellowed and swore by his dead mother that, if Nyasha was going to behave like a man, then he would fight her like a man! They went down on to the floor. Babmukuru punching Nyasha's face and banging it on the floor, screaming that he would kill her with his bare hands; Nyasha screaming and wiggling and doing what damage she could.

Finally, her mother and her brother separated them and Nyasha again went outside to smoke. What aggravated the situation this time was Nyasha hitting her father back! It was bad enough for her to talk back and argue but it was manly for her to hit him, hence his snorting, "If she is going to behave like a man . . ." Here again, the female factor came into play. Perhaps Babamukuru would accept a blow from his son but not from his daughter. After the fight with her father, Nyasha was given fourteen strokes of the cane, one stroke for every year of her life. From that incident she saw the condition of women as hopeless. From that point on, "She was retreating into some private world that we could not reach," Tambu commented. Nyasha was torn between self-autonomy and surrender. Tambu tried to counsel her by sharing her own experience with her own parents. Nyasha responded: "I know, it's the same everywhere. But he has no right to treat me like that, as though I am water to be poured wherever he wants. I know I should trust and obey and all that, but really, he hasn't the right." For Nyasha, it's a question of human right. It has nothing to do with "Englishness" any more. She tried to make Tambu see her point:

"When you've seen different things you want to be sure you're adjusting to the right thing. You can't go on all the time being whatever's necessary. You've got to have some conviction, and I'm convinced I don't want to be anyone's underdog. It's not right for anyone to be that. But once you get used to it, well, it just seems natural . . . And that's the end of you. You're trapped."

Most unfortunately for Nyasha, her father failed to recognize that her problems were real. He made no concession to the changes that took place in his children's lives and in their ways of thinking and acting. His effort to bring Nyasha back on course gave Nyasha the impression of being trapped just as her mother was trapped. Hence, when her mother finally found the courage to go away for a few days, Nyasha was comforted and she considered her mother's temporary "escape" as emancipation. She talked to Tambu about her feelings: "Sometimes I feel I'm trapped by that man, just like she is. But now she's done it, now she's broken out, I know it's possible, so I can wait."

In addition to the anguish she was suffering at home, Nyasha was isolated at school. Her mates thought she was arrogant and showy in her clothing and carriage. The isolation got worse when Tambu left for the boarding school at Sacred Heart. Nyasha had nobody to talk to or laugh with. In her letter to Tambu, she bared her soul:

I find it more and more difficult to speak with the girls at school. They resent the fact that I do not read their romance stories . . . I am convinced they have other reasons for disapproving of me. They do not like my language, my English because it is authentic and my Shona because it is not! They think I am a snob, that I think I am superior to them because I do not feel inferior to men. And all because I beat the boys in Maths! I very much would like to belong, Tambu, but I find I do not.

Like any normal teenager, Nyasha wanted to belong to the group. Being rejected by one's peers does a lot of psychic damage to a young person in particular. Nyasha faced hostility from several fronts and with her only moral supporter gone, she was bound to break down. And to avoid breaking down she tried a new approach to peaceful co-existence with her father.

Thus, she spent much of her time reading and studying. The result of her self seclusion she tells Tambu is, "Your uncle is pleased with the quieter environment . . . it is restful to have him pleased . . . I am doing my best not to antagonise him. I cannot help thinking that what antagonizes is the fact that I am me-hardly the ideal daughter for a hallowed headmaster, a revered patriarch."

Her efforts at peace not withstanding, her father would not let up with his relentless threats and orders unless Nyasha obeyed. As the leader of his community Babamukuru felt obligated to raise perfect children. Therefore, as his daughter, Nyasha must adhere to specific codes of conduct in every aspect of human behavior such as dressing, speaking, eating and so on. Yet, adhering to any type of code runs counter to the spontaneous nature of Nyasha's character; it was simply muzzling up her personality. In the end, human nature took over because a person could only take so much. Therefore, a crack occurred in her psyche. Nyasha retreated into herself. She ate less and less until she became anorexic. Despite the visible changes in her physique, her father seemed not to care. Thus, when Tambu returned from Sacred Heart she was shocked to see the bubbly Nyasha turned into a wobbly skeleton. Tambu was frightened and horrified. "Did he not know? Did he not see? She asked no one in particular. Tambu could not ask her uncle these questions, instead she begged him not to take her to the village for the holiday as he was planning to. She wanted to stay with Nyasha, to watch her and care for her. She was allowed to stay.

But nothing could stop the rapid deterioration of her cousin's condition. One evening at supper, Nyasha passed out into her plate. As usual, her father lost patience and ordered her to go to her room. Nyasha never walked out of her room on her own feet again. She lost her mental balance. She became delirious and all the bottled up emotions exploded. Nyasha started speaking the language of the possessed and accompanied it with activities of the insane. She rampaged and trashed her room. She shredded and broke anything she laid hands on, jabbing the fragments into her flesh. She spoke as she tore her room down:

Their history. Fucking liars. Their bloody lies. They've trapped us. But I won't be trapped. I'm not a good girl. I won't be trapped. I don't hate you Daddy. They want me to, but I won't. Look what they've done to us. I'm not one of them but I'm not one of you. There's a whole lot more. There's nearly a century of it. I'm afraid. It upsets people. So I need to go somewhere where it's safe . . . Somewhere where people won't mind."

Nyasha was rushed to a psychiatrist who quickly declared that Nyasha could not be ill because Africans did not suffer in that way, only white people did. Nyasha asked to see an African psychiatrist but there was none. She was persuaded to see another white psychiatrist who was more sympathetic. Nyasha was admitted to a clinic where she remained for several weeks receiving medical attention. Although her condition slowly improved, Nyasha was not completely cured. "All I knew was that the doctor would not commit himself. Nyasha's progress was still in the balance," Tambu said.

Tambu tried to figure out how all this could have happened to someone like Nyasha who supposedly had everything going for her. She could not find any explanation. However, when she told her mother what happened to Nyasha, her mother was quick with an explanation:

"It's the Englishness. It'll kill them all if they aren't careful. Look at them. That boy Chido can hardly speak a word of

Shona . . . You'll see, his children will be worse. Both of them, it's the Englishness. It's a wonder it hasn't affected the parents too."

Indeed, Tambu's illiterate mother is partially correct in attributing Nyasha's breakdown to Englishness or Assimilation. For, Nyasha had earlier admitted to her hybridity, her confusion and her inability to align herself to African or Western culture.

What is very remarkable in Nyasha's case is that she is the first female character in African literature to be so vocal and reactionary towards the tragic consequences of assimilation. She is also the first female casualty whose condition was made public. There had been the Samba Diallos, the Obi Okonkwos and numerous other male victims of assimilation, but there had never been any Nyashas.

By the tragic nature of her fate, Nyasha draws our attention to one more ignored or unrecognized aspect of womanbeing. As a female, she was not expected to feel the negative impact of uprooting. After all, a woman is born to be uprooted and moved all over the place, without injury to her original being. Even if she experienced any trauma in the process of transplantation, she's not expected to allow anyone notice it. Just as the white psychiatrist stated, Africans are not expected to be mentally agitated or unbalanced by such minor incidents as culture shocks! And by Africans he meant men! And here we have Nyasha, a girl? Give her a break!

All in all, Nyasha is a cautionary tale, a warning to all females who would dare to claim equality with men, in thought, word and deed. Nyasha paid the ultimate price for consistently flaunting her penchant for egalitarianism. She did not want to be anybody's under dog nor did she want anybody to be her under dog. To her, it was unjust for a human being to kneel in order to address another human being, no matter the status of the person kneeling. It was unfair to lionize and make a hero of a person for doing his or her duty towards a fellow human being. Yet her educated father had accepted inequality and hero worship as a way of life. Nyasha's condemnation of her father's "unjust" practices was considered another act of rebellion against constituted authority.

Because Nyasha refused to be stripped of her authentic self, she was severally victimized. But her femaleness was the central target that, like a magnet, attracted all the darts aimed at her person. Nyasha fought valiantly to retain her unique self. Yet, her collapse due to excessive social, emotional and mental pressures only proved that in spite of her hyper womanself, she was purely human. Nyasha might not have been literally killed by her father, but he caused an irreversible damage to her psychic health and mental wellbeing.

ULTRA WOMANSELF: PILATE

Pilate Dead, the most bizarre character in *Song of Solomon* is the model for Toni Morrison's gender-balanced person. By gender-balanced I mean, possessing in right proportions, both male and female essences in one body. A person so constituted could comfortably do what is normally expected of a man as well as what is expected of a woman. In other words, Pilate can act like a man or a woman depending on the situation. For instance, when Pilate locked Reba's boyfriend in a chokehold with a knife stuck into his chest as she admonished him, Pilate did what society expected only a man to do. Or, when she put on her "Aunt Jemima" act at the police station so as to retrieve her sack of bones, Pilate acted just as any helpless old woman would act. Both gestures came naturally to her. Pilate exhibited other behaviors associated with men. For instance, a man is expected to endure emotion-wrenching experiences with a straight face and without tears. The only time that Pilate was known to have shed tears was when Circe brought her cherry jam for breakfast; she was twelve and she preferred the fresh fruits she picked from her own trees. In all the heart wrenching—experiences of rejection, humiliation and jeers, Pilate endured all of them stoically and in 1963, when she was sixty-eight years old, she had not shed a tear. Pilate faced life like a soldier marching to war; she was not intimidated by death, what with her ability to communicate with her dead father.

As if to emphasize her manly features, Pilate has an imposing "unwomanly" height. For instance, when Milkman first saw her, he was so fascinated that he couldn't extricate himself from Pilate's presence: Of course, she was anything but pretty, yet he knew he could have watched her all day. Pilate did not fit the picture that people painted of her. Her fingernails were ivory white. She was unkempt but not dirty. Her berry-black lips made her look as though she wore make-up . . . And when she stood up, he all but gasped. She was as tall as his father, head and shoulders taller than himself . . . He could see her unlaced men's shoes and the silvery brown skin of her ankles.

Her manly features and actions notwithstanding, Pilate possessed the nurturing and caring attributes of the ideal mother. She provided for her children and indulged them as best she could. Her presence was soothing hence Milkman was drawn to her as to a magnate. And there was her signature song, like a family history book. Pilate was the griot of the Solomon lineage.

Toni Morrison created Pilate to be the concrete illustration of her theory of gender balance. However, the main thrust of her theory was on complementary roles of male and female in raising a family and preserving the community. Morrison was exhorting black men not to abandon their women like their ancestor Solomon abandoned Ryna and their twenty-one children. She was appealing to them to "come home" to the family and join their women in raising their children. Though the women might feel capable of heading their families, Morrison knew that men and women needed one another for emotional and psychic balance. As if to underscore her theory, Morrison's gender balanced Pilate had neither a husband nor a live-in companion. Perhaps it was the desire for male presence in the family that forced Pilate to go in search of her brother.

Pilate made her entry in the novel during the exciting moments preceding Mr. Smith's fatal attempt to fly. Three individuals stood out in the pandemonium that broke loose in front of No—Mercy Hospital. They were, Mr. Smith who was getting ready to fly off the hospital roof, Ruth Foster-Dead who was suffering labor pains at the door of the hospital and a "singing woman" whose powerful contralto distracted the children. To show the reader a better picture of the singing woman, the author presented her as a foil to the properly and neatly dressed pregnant Ruth:

The singer was as poorly dressed as the doctor's daughter was well dressed. The latter had on a neat gray coat with the traditional pregnant-woman bow at her navel, a black cloche, and a pair of four-button ladies' galoshes. The singing woman wore a knitted navy cap pulled far down over her forehead. She had wrapped herself up in an old quilt instead of a winter coat.

The author's identification of the singing woman via her clothing is deliberate. It plays on the public's image-conscious mind-set. It plays on the public's prejudicial and stereotypical equation of clothing with character. Thus, from the description, the reader concludes that the singing woman is poor and irresponsibly untraditional. But the reader would soon discover that the singing woman's manner of clothing is a bold display of her defiant attitude toward a narrow-minded and mean-spirited society. She might be poor and unconventional in certain things but she was definitely very traditional in things that mattered in life. In the end Pilate emerges as the best illustration of an ultra womanself. She transcends the definition of womanslf given at the beginning of the study.

Despite her poor untraditional attire or because of it, the singing woman caught the attention of the nurse who was trying to bring some order to the chaotic atmosphere. The nurse was searching the faces of people around her "until she saw a stout woman who looked as though she might move the earth if she wanted to.

Pilate Dead was the stout woman whose poor clothing belied her imposing and powerful personality. And yes, she could move the earth if she wanted. In her quiet but dignified manner, Pilate walked over to the woman in labor to support and reassure her:

"You should make yourself warm," she whispered to her, touching her lightly on the elbow. "A little bird'll be here with the morning."

"Oh, tomorrow morning?"

"That's the only morning coming."

"It can't be, it's too soon"

"No it ain't. Right on time."

In that short exchange, a great deal is revealed about Pilate's character. She is very confident in her knowledge of pregnancy and delivery. To begin with, her unquestionable expertise in traditional medicine made it possible for Ruth to get pregnant with this very baby. That same expertise saved the fetus from being aborted by Macon and Ruth. In that short exchange we see Pilate's caring nature and we see her loyalty to family. In her song which she picked up again after the short exchange, we see her deep rooting in oral tradition. Indeed, it would be through the same song that she passed down to her daughter and granddaughter, that Milkman would decode their common ancestry and family history. In short, Pilate was no ordinary poorly clad fellow; she was a repository of tradition!

The circumstances of Pilate's birth preceded her manner of clothing in setting her apart from other humans. The very fact that Pilate came into the world all by herself, without human intervention, conferred on her the quality of a supernatural being. After her mother died while giving birth to her, "she had come struggling out of the womb without help from throbbing muscles or pressure of swift womb water. She had inched her way headfirst out of a still, silent, and indifferent cave of flesh, dragging her own cord and her own afterbirth behind her. After the umbilical cord was cut, it healed without leaving a visible scar. To Pilate's brother, Macon who witnessed the miraculous birth of his sister, the cutting of the cord and its healing, the absence of scar to mark the navel spot, was not strange. However, to all others who had no knowledge of her birth history, Pilate was a freak of nature. "It was the absence of navel that convinced people that she had not come into this world through normal channels; had never lain, floated, or grown in some warm and liquid place connected by a tissue-thin tube to a reliable source of human nourishment."

The eventual emergence of Pilate's ultra womanself would be a direct result of the absence of a navel on her tummy. Pilate lived like any other normal child with her father and brother on their farm. Her life and her brother's life changed when their father was murdered by their white neighbors who annexed their land. Now orphaned, Pilate twelve and Macon sixteen, escaped from their farm and wandered off into the wild. While she and her brother were taking shelter in a cave, they had a fight and they ended up going their separate ways. Years later, after she came to settle in the same town as her brother, Pilate told her nephew Milkman how she became estranged from her brother:

I was cut off from people early. You can't know what that was like. After my papa was blown off that fence, me and Macon wandered around for a few days until we had a falling out and I went off on my own. I was about twelve, I think. When I cut out by myself, I headed for Virginia. I thought I remembered that was where my papa had people.

Along the way, Pilate took shelter and day jobs from people she did not know. First, she was given room and board in exchange for miscellaneous services by a preacher and his wife. They sent her to school where she felt out of place because she was much older than her classmates. However, she liked school because she discovered her love for Geography, a love that earned her a gift of a geography book from her teacher. That geography book became her most valued possession; it came to symbolize her strong sense of place. Unfortunately, the preacher developed sexual interest in her. The innocent Pilate "was so dumb I didn't know enough to stop him. But his wife caught him at it, thumbing my breasts, and put me out. I took my geography book off with me."

She joined a band of migrant workers who treated her well. She stayed with them for three years, moving from city to city. It was at that time that she learned a great deal about traditional healing from an elderly woman that she identified as a "root worker." Pilate felt at home with them because the old woman "taught me a lot and kept me from missing my own family, Macon and papa." Pilate became intimate with a fifteen-year old nephew of the root worker. One day, the boy innocently told a group of men (and women eavesdropping) that Pilate didn't have a navel. The old woman was unbelieving so she called Pilate and made her lift her dress, exposing her smooth stomach. And then her eyes flew wide open and she put her hand over her mouth. Pilate leaped up thinking a snake or a poisonous spider had crawled over her legs. "What? What is it?" she asked the old woman. "Nothing" she replied. "Child, where's your navel?" she asked Pilate. Hearing the word, navel for the first time, Pilate had no idea what the woman was talking about. So, the woman uncovered her own stomach and pointed at her navel saying, "You know, this."

What a revelation! Pilate had always assumed that her smooth stomach was one more way a girl's body differed from a boy's. Her only frame of reference was her brother; she had never seen another female's body. Still puzzled by the woman's reaction Pilate asked her what the navel was for and the woman answered: "It's for . . . it's for people who were born natural." Of course, Pilate didn't understand what the woman meant, but she was told to leave. "On account of my stomach?" she asked. With apologies, they sent Pilate away with more money than she had earned. They pitied her but were terrified for having been in the company of something God never made.

Pilate joined another group of migrant workers heading towards Virginia. Once more, she took a man to bed and was "expelled" again, on account of her stomach. This time however, the group simply hurried away while she was in town doing a little shopping. This was the turning point for Pilate. Now that her innocence of her physical body had been shattered, she must find a way to prevent "normal people" from chasing her away from the human community. She must now allow her true self to emerge, for she had been holding it back as she struggled for a foothold in society. Pilate sort of said, "To hell with normalcy and conventions. I will be myself and live by own rules." From this time forward, Pilate would do whatever was necessary for her physical and emotional survival. She would do whatever gave her satisfaction regardless of people's reaction to her appearance and behavior.

Thus, after the group took off without her, she went ahead to look for shelter and for job. She walked into a laundry mart of sorts and asked to spend the night there. The next morning she was hired as a washerwoman. She worked and slept there and saved her earnings. When she saved enough money she took the train to Virginia. She was unable to locate anyone who might have known her family. Her family name was troubling to people, so, whenever she asked about Dead's family "people frowned and said, 'No, never heard of any such.'" When she heard of a farming community in an island off the coast of Virginia; she decided to go there. She persuaded the ferryman to take her there for five cents. On reaching there, she was "employed" by a family when she explained that she wasn't afraid of work and that she liked rural life.

Pilate did whatever job was assigned to her. She now knew to hide her stomach to avoid frightening people and getting herself rejected. Now sixteen, she took a lover and contrived a way to hide her stomach from him. She succeeded in getting pregnant but shocked the people when she refused to marry her lover. She knew she could not hide her stomach forever from a husband. The people accepted her and treated her well till she had her baby. To her relief, the midwife did not notice her "deformity" because she was too busy attending to her delivery. Pilate was very happy when she saw that her baby had a navel! Following her family tradition, she asked for a bible so that she could choose a name for her baby. There was no bible so she asked for a biblical name for a girl. She was given several from which she chose Rebecca, and shortened it to Reba.

When Reba turned two, Pilate left with her and started roaming the country, living a bohemian life style for about twenty years. She had relations with men all along but none was as good as the one she had with Reba's father on the island.

Finally, Pilate got fed up with people's reaction to her smooth stomach. It was as if she had finally come of age. She decided to stop worrying about people and their reactions to her. She stopped hiding her stomach. She became aware of the "gravity" of her deformity; that men were so frightened and put off by it that they would rather mate with all sorts of deformed or depraved people, even with animals, than with her. She realized that she could not marry and keep a husband; she could not have lengthy relationships with men. Moreover, women whispered and pulled their children away at her approach. Her lack of navel would isolate her from people forever?

Finally Pilate began to take offense . . . When she realized what her situation in the world was and would probably always be, she threw away every assumption she had learned and began at zero.

She had to sort out her priorities in life. She must find out the sources of her happiness and sadness. She must decide what was valuable to her. She must find out what she needed to have or do to stay alive. While she was seeking to understand her needs, she found there was nothing out there to be afraid of, not even death. After all, she had been communicating with her dead father.

The first act of her freedom was to cut off her hair. She stared at people, but never made impolite observations. She was generous with her food. And she gave up, apparently, all interest in table manners or hygiene but acquired a deep concern for and about human relationships. It is strange that Pilate cared deeply for human relationship considering the numerous occasions that people excluded her from their company. Again, her insistence on human relationship was one more way that she proved her superiority to "regular" people.

As if to test her new freedom and defiance of social norms, Pilate settled on bootlegging as a means of income. She set up her own rules for her business. She did not drink and she did not allow her clients to drink on her premises. In that way, she avoided troubles associated with brewing and selling illicit liquor.

When her daughter Reba had her own daughter, Hagar, Pilate provided for them too. Her sense of family was very strong and because of her granddaughter she decided to go in search of her brother Macon. Pilate knew that wherever her brother was, he would be prosperous, conventional, more like the things and people Hagar seemed to admire. More importantly, she wanted to make peace with her brother.

With plenty of money from her liquor brewing business, Pilate and her family set out in search of her brother. However, when she found Macon he was very inhospitable, embarrassed and unforgiving. Pilate would have moved on, but the condition of her sister-in-law, Ruth, compelled her to do something for her. It happened that Macon had abandoned Ruth. She had been dying literally from sex starvation for twenty years! Pilate the fearless and compassionate one had to intervene and force her brother "to return" to his wife, even for a few days. Pilate brought to bear her knowledge of traditional medicine. She concocted some mixture for Ruth and told her what to do to make her husband come to her. The experiment or rather the "voodoo" worked. Macon came to his wife for four days in a row. A month later, Ruth found herself pregnant. Macon was furious and he tried everything possible to make his wife abort the fetus. Again, Pilate intervened to save the pregnancy. She laid down rules for Ruth to follow and prescribed "stuff" for her to eat to control nausea. She even gave her some contraption to wear below the waistline to hold the stomach up till the baby came.

It was during the exciting moments preceding the birth of Ruth's baby boy, a baby that owed its conception and birth to Pilate, that the latter was presented to the reader for the first time. Pilate was singing her signature song: O Sugarman done fly away, Sugarman done gone, Sugarman cut across the sky, Sugarman gone home . . . It was from that point that her eccentric ways began to be pointed out to the reader. It was her eccentricity that embarrassed her brother and caused him to flee from her as from the plague.

However, what Macon and other people saw as odd or unnatural behavior was nothing more than Pilate's demonstration of her freedom as an individual. When people tried to exclude her from their midst, Pilate refused to budge. Instead of allowing people to hound her out of their midst, she staked her claim to a space in society. She created her own way of living and forced society to let her be and live on her own terms. Hence, Pilate and her daughter and granddaughter, lived in a single story house whose setup was quite unconventional:

She had no electricity because she would not pay for the service, nor for gas. At night she and her daughter lit the house with candles and kerosene lamps. They warmed themselves and cooked with wood and coal, pumped kitchen water into a dry sink through a pipeline from a well and lived pretty much as though progress was a word that meant walking a little farther on down the road."

Only a person of extraordinary courage would go to the extreme that Pilate went in her defiance of social norms and public opinion. From her personal appearance, to her living arrangement, to her food and feeding habits, Pilate was in a world of her own. As Macon secretly observed, Pilate and her daughters ate like children. Whatever they had a taste for. No meal was ever planned or balanced or served. Nor was there any gathering at the table . . . They ate what they had or came across or had a craving for. Pilate was content in the way she lived her life. She did not go crawling to her brother for handouts. Instead, her house was open to anyone who needed food or shelter.

In the end, society grudgingly came to terms with Pilate's unconventional ways. In fact, there seemed to exist, an unwritten agreement whereby people respected her space and idiosyncrasies and nobody dared to "cross" her. Thus, one day, a reckless boyfriend of Reba's nearly got himself killed by Pilate, when he brazenly attacked and hurt Reba in her mother's back yard. When Hagar told Pilate that the young man was beating Reba, Pilate took a kitchen knife and snuck up on him:

Approaching him from the back, she whipped her right arm around his neck and positioned the knife at the edge of his heart. She waited until the man felt the knife point before she jabbed it skillfully, about a quarter of an inch through his shirt into the skin. Still holding his neck, so he couldn't see but could feel the blood making his shirt sticky, she talked to him. "Now, I'm not going to kill you, honey. Don't you worry none . . ."

After admonishing the man for daring to beat up a weak woman, she let him go. The neighbors had gathered in Pilate's yard to watch the drama:

They knew right away that the man was a new comer to the city. Otherwise he would have known not to fool with anything that belonged to Pilate, who never bothered anybody, was helpful to everybody, but who also was believed to have the power to step out of her skin, set a bush afire from fifty yards, and turn a man into a ripe rutabaga-all on account of the fact that she had no navel. So, they didn't have much sympathy for him.

This incident touched directly on Pilate's strong sense of family. Despite her early breakup with her brother, Pilate always tried to hold on to family ties. To her, those ties should be constantly strengthened and if possible, extended ad infinitum. It was for that reason that she picked up after more than twenty years to look for her brother so as to reunite their family. Her loyalty to family included their dead members, hence her constant communication with her dead father. It was in obedience to her father's command that she carried with her, the presumed skeleton of a strange white man that Macon had presumably killed when they took shelter inside a cave. However, by some extraordinary fluke, the bones turned out to be her father's. Pilate's sack of bones that she called her inheritance would play a role that would change the course of the story. Pilate's inheritance that Macon took to be gold would finally lead to a search that would in turn lead to the discovery of their true ancestry. It would lead to Milkman rethinking his priorities and discovering the importance of family.

Of all the values that Pilate cherished, love was paramount. Pilate's love and compassion for other human beings speak to her humanism. For, only a person of her caliber could rise above the type of prejudice and rejection that she had to deal with for most of her life. Though not known for her Christian religious practice, Pilate's understanding of love closely followed Christ's teaching on the subject. Pilate had a great capacity for love and she even extended love to her enemies. For instance, her brother viewed and treated her as an enemy. Yet, she took the initiative to find him so as to reconcile with him. When Macon rejected her peace overtures, Pilate did not walk away in anger. Instead, she was saddened by the hate she noticed between Macon and his wife. Pilate worked "miracles," to bring husband and wife together for a spell of passionate loving. It was the loving that resulted in a male heir for Macon.

Though Macon banned her from his home and forbade his wife and children from interacting with her, Pilate's home was open to them as to everyone else. When Milkman disobeyed his father and went to Pilate's house with Guitar, he was pleasantly surprised by the warm treatment he received from Pilate. He wondered why his father sternly warned him to keep away from Pilate:

"I don't want you over there."

"Why? You still haven't said why."

"Just listen to what I say. That woman's no good. She's a snake, and can charm you like a snake, but still a snake."

"You talking about your own sister, the one you carried in your arms to the fields every morning."

"That was a long time ago. You seen her. What she look like to you? Somebody nice? Somebody normal? Or somebody cut your throat?"

"She didn't look like that, Daddy."

"Well, she is like that."

"What'd she do?"

"It ain't what she did; it's what she is."

"What is she?"

"A snake, I told you."

Macon's threats and orders to keep away from Pilate made Milkman more determined to spend time in her house. From the first time he set eyes on Pilate, Milkman seemed to be drawn to her. Because of the role she played in Milkman's birth, Pilate had a special place for him in her heart. Eventually Milkman became a regular visitor to Pilate's house. During a conversation with his father, Milkman told Macon of a curious green sack containing Pilate's inheritance, hanging in the middle of Pilate's room. Instantly Macon concluded that the sack contained the gold they saw in the cave when they took shelter there. Macon saw an opportunity for turning Milkman into an enemy of Pilate. He persuaded Milkman to go and steal Pilate's "inheritance." They would share the booty and Milkman could then leave home to "find himself."

The burglary landed Milkman and his accomplice, Guitar at the police station. Pilate's reaction to the burglary and its perpetrators was an unmistakable demonstration of showing love to one's enemies. Instead of denouncing the thieves and screaming for justice, Pilate put up a well-rehearsed "Aunt Jemima" act that let the thieves off the hook while restoring her inheritance to her. In short, Pilate interceded for her enemies. Her gesture left Milkman utterly confused. How could Pilate humiliate herself to save him from prosecution and possible imprisonment after what he had just done to her? He went over in his head what he was willing to do to steal Pilate's property:

He had been prepared to knock her down if she had come into the room while he was in the act of stealing it. To knock down an old black lady who had cooked him his first perfect egg . . . She had told him stories, sung him songs, fed him bananas and corn bread. This old black lady-had brought him into the world when only a miracle could have. It was this woman who shuffled into the police station and did a little number for the cops, opening herself up wide for their amusement, their pity, their scorn, their mockery, their disbelief, their meanness, their anger, their whimsy . . . whatever would be useful to her and to himself.

How many people could put on such a humiliating act for the sake of those who meant them harm? Pilate demonstrated her superhuman love that forgave all wrongs. Pilate was shot and killed by Guitar, the enemy that she had humiliated herself to save from prosecution and incarceration. In her dying words, Pilate expressed her limitless capacity to love. As she took her last breath, she said to Milkman: "Watch Reba for me. I wish I'd a knowed more people. I would of loved 'em all. If I'd a knowed more, I would a loved more."

Considering her history of being treated like some loathsome unearthly creature, of being constantly rejected, Pilate was a perfect candidate for self hate or even suicide.

Yet, those feelings never entered her mind. She might be a freak to others but she never questioned the state of her being. Even when the root worker told her that the absence of a navel rendered her "something not made by God," she was not perturbed by the revelation. Rather, she found a way to work around the condition. She found a way to conduct herself and protect people from her deformity.

Pilate's self-acceptance was perhaps the most important step towards her survival in a hostile world. For, it is only someone secure in herself that can live comfortably among people who shunned her. Only a person of Pilate's self assurance can return love and caring for hate and rejection. Pilate's kind of love might not be exactly divine, but it was certainly spiritual. Pilate's self-acceptance and the choices she made and acted upon put her in a unique class of an ultra womanself.

IMPREGNABLE WOMANSELF: SILLA & SELINA

I n her masterpiece novel, *Brown Girl, Brownstones*, Paule Marshall presents Silla and her daughter Selina. This mother and daughter are a perfect example of the cliché—like mother, like daughter. By Selina's own admission, she is cut from the same cloth as her mother. In what would pass for a farewell speech, before starting her journey back to her island homeland, Selina said to her mother:

"Everybody used to call me Deighton's Selina but they were wrong. Because you see I'm truly your child. Remember how you used to talk about how you left home and came here alone as a girl of eighteen and was your own woman? I used to love hearing that. And that's what I want. I want it!"

Silla recognized and affirmed Selina's "true confession" with her own confession,

"You was always too much woman for me anyway, soul. And my own mother did say two head-bulls can't reign in a flock."

Both Silla and Selina came into the world as unassailable selves. Both of them were so firmly rooted in their selfhood that their own mothers could not influence their decisions to strike out on their own, to establish and actualize themselves. At age ten, Silla was already a field hand in a sugarcane field. She worked from sunup to sundown. And when fieldwork was scarce, she would switch to hawking mangoes from the early hours of the morning till dusk. From that tender age, Silla was self-driven in her desire to make money and improve her life. At eighteen she decided to leave her homeland for the United States where there was better opportunity for wealth accumulation and self-improvement. Narrating her experiences to Selina, she recalled how she prevailed upon her mother to find the money for her to pay the fare to the USA: "No, I wun let my mother know peace till she borrow the money and send me here."

All alone in a foreign country Silla fell in love and married a fellow Bajan, Deighton Boyce. Unfortunately for Silla, her husband was a complete opposite of her. He loved the softer side of life. He was neither ambitious nor aggressive. He was simply uninterested in his people's rat racing towards the American dream. He preferred spending his money on himself. Silla's efforts to pull him up and drag him along her money-grabbing path failed. "For years now I been trying to put little ambition in that man but he ain interested in making a head way," she complained to her friend Virgie. Eventually, Deighton became a sort of millstone fastened to Silla's ankles to prevent any forward movements. But Silla,s type of self was unstoppable. If anything, impediments sharpened her resolve to achieve whatever she set her mind to. Like most Jamaican immigrants in New York, Silla had set her goal to eventually own, refurbish and rent out rooms in the run-down brownstone building where she formerly lived as a tenant. To achieve this goal, she cleaned houses in Jewish homes on weekdays. On weekends, she baked and prepared several Jamaican dishes that she sold for extra income. Despite her hard work and serious saving, Silla's money wasn't adding up fast enough. Unlike other husbands, Deighton was not contributing to the family funds. Instead, he squandered his money on fine clothing, on his mistresses and on dead-end programs that he hoped would lead to high-paying blue collar jobs.

As his luck would have it, Deighton's sister died back home and left him a piece of land. Deighton was very pleased with his land that measured about two acres and he started fantasizing about a house he would build on it. Silla was beside herself with anger and envy. She could never understand the workings of providence. Addressing no one in particular, she spoke out loud:

"Look how it does come . . . What is it, that does give what little luck there is to fools . . . ? Not a soul ever give me nothing a-tall, a-tall. I always had to make my own luck. And look at he! Somebody dead so and he got ground so. Got land now!"

Silla felt deeply hurt by Deighton's inheritance because she knew that he was not going to put the land to any profitable use for the family. He had already indicated that he wasn't going to sell the land. He would rather enjoy a life-long fantasy of the house he was going to build on his piece of land. But Silla knew her husband too well to entertain any hopes that he would do anything concrete with the land. On her part, Silla knew that she was going to do something with that land. When Virgie asked what she was going to do she replied, "I don know, soul. I don know. But mark muh words, I ain gon rest good till I do something." As several Bajan couples bought and rented out their own refurbished brownstone buildings, Silla agonized over the useless piece of land in the homeland. One day, while listening to Iris recite the names of new homeowners in their community, Silla shouted, "Oh God, I can get the money!" "What, Dear-heart? What money?" Iris asked. "From the land. I gon sell it," Silla replied. Her friends teased her and asked if she was going to use voo-doo on Deighton since he wouldn't sell the land otherwise. Silla swore:

"Be-Jesus-Christ, I gon do that for him then. Even if I got to see my soul fall howling into hell I gon do it. As God is my witness I know how to sell it for him . . . Everybody buying and I still leasing? Oh no, Florrie. I gon fix he and fix he good. I gon show the world that Silla ain nice!"

Consequently, Silla set up an elaborate plan to sell the land behind Deighton's back. She learned to use the typewriter to avoid detection through handwriting. Passing herself up as her husband, Silla maintained months of regular correspondence with her sister-in-law during which she left no doubts in her sister-in-law's mind that she had been corresponding with her brother. In the end, Silla convinced her sister-in-law to sell the land for her brother. The land fetched nine hundred dollars. It was a perfect crime except for a simple mistake-the check was made out to Deighton! Silla congratulated herself for her dubious victory as she awaited the arrival of the check in the mail. Though apprehensive that she could convince Deighton to cash and hand over the money to her for a down payment on the building she wanted to purchase, she did not despair. She would find a way to make her husband cooperate. On the eve of Deighton's trip to cash the check, Silla played her role as a good loving wife. She and Deighton had a romantic evening that ended in a romantic night in bed together! It was at this moment of renewed intimacy that Deighton convinced his wife not to accompany him to the bank the following morning. And Silla would live to regret the carnal weakness that led her to agree with her husband's decision to go to the bank alone!

For what seemed like an eternity, Silla nervously waited for Deighton's return from the bank. Selina tried to reassure her that her father would return. Meanwhile, Silla wallowed in self loathing and regret:

Oh God! . . . How could I let a smile . . . ? A smile now and a few words and thing in the night . . . Judas smile! Judas words! To let a Judas smile win out . . . To let the man walk out this house with the draft big in his hand and the false smile on his lips and know deep within muh it was wrong and still let he go . . . Oh God, a few words in the night . . . I din know I could still get so foolish . . . Silla was at the point of resigning herself to the fact that Deighton had run away with the cash when his voice burst in the dark hall like a light suddenly beamed across a night sky—gay, teasing, ebullient, shouting, 'Where's everybody? Where's muh lady-folks? Come, Selina! Come, Ina! Light, light, let there be light, it say in the good book . . . Deighton made his way into the living room, laden with his purchases. His daughters stood aghast, his wife stood paralyzed with anger trapped inside of her. "It Christmas in the middle of March. I coming through" he announced. "There's somethin' fuh everybody today . . . somethin' fuh ev . . . very . . . body," he chanted and pranced about. It was a triumphant chant of an underdog having the last laugh.

Still relishing his "victory" Deighton distributed the expensive dresses and coats he had squandered the cash on.

He ended with a flourish, brandishing his shiny trumpet that cost over three hundred dollars! Deighton fitted the trumpet to his lips and played a few false notes. Remembering that he had not given Silla her own gift, he tore the trumpet from his lips and cried, "Silla! Silla-gal, I almost forgot yuh. I sorry . . ." Awakening from her stupor, Silla's lips formed the words, "Over nine . . . hundred . . . odd dollars cash . . ." Deighton continued teasing her: "Lord-God, woman, nine hundred dollars ain no money out there on Fifth Avenue in New York . . . But come, don fret, girl. I come back din I? And I even bring somethin' for you and all. You did think I forgot you but I didn't . . ." From a large box Deighton withdrew a bold-red coat with a collar of dark fur. Holding it out to Silla he asked "How's this, Silla-gal? Yuh like it. I did always tell you that red suit your skin. So catch, girl!" He threw the coat and it fell at Silla's feet. "Pick it up, Silla-gal! Pick it up and know that they ain penny one left to buy another one. That's it. That's the last of the over nine hundred odd dollars cash lying there!"

As his family stood dazed by the drama, Deighton carried on teasing and taunting his wife. Finally he picked up his trumpet and started towards his room to practice. As he neared Silla, he made an elaborate bow. Silla's pent-up anger burst and she lunged and wrenched the trumpet from him. She struck it once to the floor, breaking it. Then she rhythmically smashed it to pieces. It was Deighton's turn to be dazed. However, his amazement turned into amusement, and with a derisive laughter he gasped: "Woman, it insured. What you wasting energy for? There's plenty more where that come from. It insured!" Silla retorted: "I'll get the house despite you! I'll buy it yet!"

Deighton shot back:

Why not? There's plenty of loan sharks out there on Fulton Street waiting for you house-hungry Bajans . . . Why not? You can buy it tomorrow-self. And Silla-gal, it will be yours. Only your name 'pon the paper, and you wun have to worry 'bout my selling it behind your back." Silla's retort stung the air:

I'll get it. And as God is my witness I gon get you too. And I wun make mistakes this time. I wun let a Judas smile and Judas words in the night and the thing so turn me foolish. You could touch me and it would be like touching stone. Nothing, nothing gon stop me. I gon steel my heart and bide my time and see you dead-dead at my feet! Deighton shuddered at Silla's words for he knew that she was not bluffing. He in turn steeled his heart to receive whatever blow Silla was going to land on him. Smiling, he said to Silla, "You's God, you must know," He went away teasing and taunting Silla, whose lips continued moving in an endless chant, "Over . . . nine . . . hundred odd . . . dollars cash . . . . over . . . nine hundred odd dollars cash throw 'way."

Deighton's revenge was only a temporary set back for Silla. If anything, the setback fired her resolve to purchase the building in which she now rented an apartment. But she must punish Deighton for the disgrace his action brought to her family; she must punish him for making her an object of pity in the Bajan community. She vowed to bide her time and see Deighton "dead-dead at my feet." Thanks to a pseudo divine intervention, Silla didn't have to wait long to deal her death—blow on Deighton. In a factory accident, Deighton's arm was caught in a new machine he was trying to operate; the nerves were severed. When Silla went to see him at the hospital he turned his face to the wall. The only thing he said to her was to tell his daughters not to come and see him at the hospital. He

161

could not stand their seeing him in his moment of weakness. Silla was genuinely saddened by the event. She seemed to regret her desire for vengeance. She spoke aloud to herself: "Be-Christ, you does ask for vengeance and sometime the sight of it when it comes does make you wish different . . ."

While he was in the hospital, Deighton joined a religious cult run by a man known as Father Peace. He had encountered the cult through an old newspaper he found in his hospital locker. Deighton's conversion was so thorough that he abandoned his family and moved to the establishment of the cult. That was the breaking point in his humiliation, not only of himself but also of his entire family. And it was the last straw for Silla. The shame of the wasted nine hundred dollars was still fresh and now this! Her pride was terribly hurt, especially in the Bajan community where other women looked up to her. The ridicule and embarrassment would be too much for her to bear. The only way to minimize the damage would be to send Deighton back to their island homeland. Consequently, Silla called the immigration to come and arrest her husband, an illegal alien! When she finally led the officer to Deighton's new place of residence, Silla shouted in a voice full of rage: That's he, officer. That's he, I say. His own don't count since he take up with this bogus god, so let him go back where he come from! He don need nobody now but Father? He's happy? Well, le's see how happy he gon be back home!" As Deighton failed to respond to the officer's questions, Silla continued, "That's he. That's his name. His head turn, officer, and he don even know himself anymore . . ."

It took a rough and vigorous shaking by the policeman to rouse Deighton from his trans-like state and he said, "Yes, officer, they did call me Deighton Boyce." As he was being led away, he stopped in front of Silla and they both searched each other's face. There was the same love in their eyes, the one they felt when they first met. Silently they asked each other what had gone wrong, what it was that had ruined them for each other, and their mutual bewilderment confessed they did not know. As he moved away, Silla's eyes followed him with enraged pity. She wept and shouted, "Let him go back where he come from if he don't count his own. Let him go back!" It was a painful cry inspired by love, not hate, not vengeance. Silla would rather live with that pain than see her husband utterly unmanned and brought so low by a dubious religious cult. The homeland would be the best asylum and shelter for him. But Deighton had a different plan. He would rather drown himself than return in shame to his homeland. Thus:

On the day the war ended, a cable arrived saying that Deighton Boyce had either jumped or fallen overboard and drowned at a point within sight of the Barbados coast and that a post-humus burial service had been read at sea.

The news of Deighton's death was devastating to Selina who refused to be comforted. She wore black clothing and mourned her father beyond the traditional one year period of mourning. Silla was equally unsettled by the news but she bore it stoically and mourned in silence. She would not give anybody the satisfaction of "catching" her grieving for her husband.

As she had vowed before Deighton, Silla now owned the brownstone building they lived in. However, owning property did not cause Silla to slow down in her money-making ventures. She found a job in a hospital after the war plant she worked in was closed down. She registered in a course in practical nursing so as to move up in her new job. At night she did her house chores and studied till she fell asleep on the books. She still prepared her native dishes on weekends and sold them to friends and neighbors. Her friend Florrie watching her kneading dough exclaimed: "I tell yuh, Silla, you's a real-real Bajan woman. You can bear up under I don know what." But her daughter Selina knew otherwise; she had been a witness to her mother's weariness as she struggled to work and study at nights.

Yet, Silla had new challenges. She wanted Selina to go to college; she must figure out how to make more rooms out of the existing rooms so as to raise more money: "If I could only make upstairs into smaller rooms and charge little more . . . But that old woman wun dead and the free-bee ain thinking about moving. But I gon start thinking hard for both of them and we gon see."

Once more, Silla who never issued empty threats swore to do something to get rid of the ailing fragile Miss Mary and Suggie the free-bee or whore, as she called her. To start with, she stormed into Mary's room not knowing that Selina was visiting as usual. On seeing her mother, Selina thought she was looking for her but she was asked instead:

But girl, what you does find in sitting up here with this rank, half dead old woman, nuh? Or with that whore next door? Why you would rather visit Thompson with that smelly life-sore on her leg than Beryl and them so? Why? I can't fathom you a-tall, a-tall."

Selina's enraged response was: "What do you want up here? Don't come in here. She's scared and she can't talk." Suddenly Silla shouted at Selina, "What it tis you does find here?" When Selina did not respond, Silla strode up to the foot of the bed and thrusting out her face, she pierced Mary's face with a terrifying stare shouting:

"But why you wun dead, nuh? What it tis you waiting on? Tell me. You can't take this old house with you. It belongs to me now. You don understand that yet? Yes, it belong to me! And I gon get you out yet. Yuh hear that? I gon call in the Board of Health to see all this dirt and get you out that way. Yes, and your long-face daughter too that never once count me to speak because my skin black. Silla literally proceeded to ransack and turn Mary's room inside out. Before she left, she went to the foot of the bed again, and with outstretched arms she pleaded: "Why you wun dead?"

A few months later Mary died; she was literally frightened to death. As she had planned, Silla created smaller rooms out of Mary's space and rented them out at exorbitant rates. She now turned her attention to her next victim, Suggie. She secured affidavits from the roomers testifying that Suggie was a prostitute and a harmful influence on Silla's two daughters. Besides, her presence lowered the value of her property. Armed with her evidence, Silla petitioned the authorities to evict Suggie and her request was granted.

As Selina watched Suggie pack her belongings, Suggie told her the charges that Silla brought against her. Turning to Selina she said: "Tell me, how I harm you. All I ever did was to give you a little rum and make jokes about loving-up and so. That's all. How's that a harmful influence? Is you a drunkard now? Is you a whore? Tell me?" With pain written all over her face Selina replied:

No, I'm not a whore and I' m not a drunkard and neither are you. It's not you, Miss Suggie. It's just that I' m to have no one, that's all. Look how she practically frightened the old lady to death . . . And now she's got this idea about filling the house with roomers to make more money for me to be something I don't want to be. But you just wait I' m going to show her.

As property owner, Silla faced a new challenge—she's inflicted with "property owner's disease." She must now deal with the frustration and anxiety of watching every move of her tenants to prevent them from damaging her property. When Florrie told her that the authorities were strict with immigrant property owners, Silla replied: "I tell yuh, I wun mind if they did take the blasted house, I' m so sick of aggravating myself with roomers." As usual, Silla remained undaunted by the new challenge of protecting her property. She had no sympathy for roomers. Instead she justified her nastiness by philosophizing on the nature of power and social climbing; both were colorblind:

People got to make their own way. And nearly always to make your way in this Christ world you got to be hard and sometimes misuse others, even your own. Oh, nobody wun admit it. We don talk about it, but we does live by it-each in his own way.

To support her claim, Silla cited the example of what she suffered when she was cleaning houses for Jewish people. She asserted that the Jews didn't misuse black people because of their color but because blacks couldn't do better. "All the time I was down on his floor I was saying to myself: 'Lord, lemme do better than this. Lemme rise!' No, power is a thing that don really have nothing to do with color . . . Power is a thing that don make you nice. But it's the way of this Christ world best proof!" Having clawed her way to the top, Silla had to scuffle to stay there. She had earlier declared that "Silla ain nice" when she swore to do something with Deighton's piece of land. Now with her own property, she had no qualms playing the dirty and ruthless game required to hold on to power.

Selina had listened to all of her mother's words with embarrassment. She was suffocating with anger, but when she caught the mother's eyes, she saw the mute plea for understanding and tolerance—not only for what she had just said but for all she had ever said or done. Silla glowered at her and ordered her to go over and join the young people in their discussion of their Association. When they asked Selina what she thought of their Association, she blasted them with her quiet but devastating response:

I think it stinks. And why does it stink? Because it's the result of living by the most shameful codes possible-dog-eat dog, exploitation, the strong over the weak, the end justifies the means-the whole kit and caboodle. Your Association? It's a band of frightened people. Clannish. Narrow-minded. Selfish. Prejudiced. Pitiful. Provincial! That's your Association.

Selina jumped out of her chair and rushed out of the room only to collide with Clive, a twenty-nine year old veteran of the Vietnam War. It was a fateful meeting of kindred spirits. They both felt alienated from their Bajan community and their values. Clive offered to walk her home. They stopped at the park and before she knew it, Selina lost her virginity that very night; she was eighteen. Meeting Clive would put a new twist to Selina's plans for the future. She thought she had found the "boy" she had been dreaming of. She set to planning their future together, away from the Bajan people. Since neither of them had the money to go away, Selina had to come up with a scheme to raise the money. Just as her mother did with her father's piece of land, Selina laid out an elaborate plan to win the scholarship money that the Bajan Association reserved for their brightest student each year.

Cloaked in false penitence and humility, Selina apologized to the Association of young Bajans and registered as a member. Very soon, she became the "think tank" of the Association. Her ideas were always the best and she practically presided over every major event of the organization; she earned their trust. She worked equally hard at school and had little doubt that she would win the scholarship. She also had no doubts that Clive would "take her away" from the Bajan community. He had been playing along with her plan to win the scholarship and use the money for their escape.

Before the winner of the scholarship was announced, Selina's plan to go away with Clive was derailed. It took a minor test of Clive's loyalty to convince Selina that Clive's mother had a stronger hold on her son than any other woman! Clive chose to answer his mother's summons that night rather than stay with his girl friend who had just undergone a traumatic racist encounter with a merciless white woman. This betrayal was unforgivable. Selina walked out of the relationship and dropped the plan of going away with Clive, but she would still go away alone.

Selina and Silla went for the scholarship award ceremony. When Selina was announced as the winner, she walked up to the table and picked up the check. However, her "acceptance" speech was unprecedented and deadly:

In one way I wish I could accept the award and use it as you would like. Because I know that's how I could best express my respect and affection. But I can't accept it-which means probably that I'll never be able to convince you how I feel now . . . I can't accept it, because I don't deserve it. And the reasons are despicable . . . Let's just say that my dedication was false and the outstanding contributions were all pretenses . . . Even my apology was phony. But I offer it again, for the last time, and mean it . . .

Everyone was stunned in disbelief. Silla's rage was indescribable and she flew at Selina shouting: Yuh lie! Lies! Poor-great! Poor-great like the father before you." But Selina hadn't finished with her revenge. She dealt Silla more deathblows with:

All right, Mother, I'll tell you even though I shouldn't. Last week I intended to take the money. But not for what you thought. Not to save for any exalted plan you had for me. I wanted it for one reason: to go away with Clive. Yes, I never stopped seeing him even though I promised. That's why I became so devoted to the Association . . . Why did I change my mind? I just couldn't . . . Something happened and I couldn't any more.

It was as if a veil had been lifted and Silla seemed to realize what hit her and she started shouting:

Spitework! Spitework, that's what it tis. Because of what I did to yuh father. All these years you been waiting to get at me. Ever since the night you did call me Hitler you been waiting. You did always think I killed him. Yes. But I din do it out of hate. I din mean to send him to his death-it's just that I cun bear to see him suffering.

Remembering her father's disgraceful death Selina lashed out at her mother; "You did it because you knew he was never coming back to you. Yes, I blamed you. In this way, Selina had her own revenge at last. Her plan to abandon college and run away with the shiftless Clive would have been more than sufficient punishment for her mother. Silla had met her match in her daughter. She had no choice but to concede defeat. Selina announced her intention to go away alone, though penniless. Silla sat down to better absorb the shock. Now, all her struggles and successes seemed worthless. With a tearful voice she mumbled:

Going'way?. One call sheself getting married and the other going'way. Gone so! They ain got no more uses for me and they gone. Oh God, is this what you does get for the nine months and the pain and the long years putting bread in their mouth? Here it tis just when I start making plans to buy a house in Crown Heights . . .

Selina snapped at her, "I' m not interested in houses!" Silla nodded bitterly and continued her plaint: "You did always scorn me for trying to get little property." But Selina said she used to scorn her for that but not any more. She had tried to explain it all to them at the award ceremony; she had tried to tell them that she did not want what they wanted. Still bitter, Silla asked her: "What it tis you want? She replied: "I don't know."

Silla accepted her daughter's decision, though she attempted to "stage" a concerned mother's protest by adding: "Girl, do you know what it tis out there? How those white people does do yuh?" Selina saw the deep sadness weighing her mother down. But, like her mother, Selina steeled her heart saying, "Mother, I have to disappoint you. Maybe it's as you once said: that in making your way you always hurt someone. I don't know . . ." It was at this juncture that she reminded her mother that she was truly her daughter, not Deighton's as everyone used to say. Suddenly, Silla envisioned her younger self now reincarnated in Selina. Her memory thrust her back to the ship as she sailed away from her homeland at eighteen.

Reluctantly, Silla waved Selina away with, "G'long. G'long! You was always too much woman for me any way, soul. And my own mother did say two head-bull can't reign in a flock. G'long! If I din dead yet, you and your foolishness can't kill muh now!"

It was just like Silla to stand defiant against any assault, physical or emotional. After all, she had bitten and survived so many obstacles on her road to self advancement and self actualization. What is one more act of desertion by a daughter she thought belonged to her alone finally? If she didn't die from previous emotional assaults, surely, this final one wouldn't kill her.

Silla's words are those of a brave person who would never shed tears in public but would let the tears freely flow inwards. As a pillar of strength and role model to other Bajan women, Silla must maintain her image of an impregnable womanself.

Silla is left alone to savor her pyrrhic victory. Had it all been worth it? Had she any regrets about the way she conducted her affairs and her life? Her final words to Selina testify to her bullish defiance of life in general. She remained unscathed by her battles against obstacles.

Silla's overpowering personality is unparalleled by any other female character in black literature. Not only did humans cower at the sight of Silla, even Nature and the Seasons were affected by Silla's presence:

Silla Boyce brought the theme of winter into the park with her dark dress amid the summer green and the bright-figured house-dresses of the women lounging on the benches there . . . Her lips, set in a permanent protest against life, implied that there was no time for gaiety. And the park, the women, the sun even gave way to her dark force; the flushed summer colors ran together and faded as she passed.

Silla was like a massive piece of machinery to her daughter. Selina came to that realization on the day she went to her mother's work place to confront her for her plans to sell her father's piece of land back home. After watching the huge machine and the workers operating it, Selina realized the machine-mass had an ugly force but it had grandeur. As she watched her mother expertly handling her own section of the machine, a fleeting notion nudged her and she perceived the resemblance between her mother and the machine. She found a perfect metaphor for her mother's being: The mother was like the machines, some larger form of life with an awesome beauty all her own. This image of a machine comes close to the impression that Silla gave people about herself. To those close to her, she was like an enormous immovable boulder. She often steeled her heart while her words of threat were set in stone! "I will get you for this, I will buy it yet! As God is my witness, when I am done with you . . ." These were some of her recurring threats and she never failed to carry them out.

From her pre-adolescent years, she had been in control of her life, and when she started her own family, she was in control of everybody in her household. Looking at her relationship with her husband, one could tell that Silla was the one who chose Deighton to be the husband that she would mold into her desired shape but fate played her false. Deighton was neither ambitious nor aggressive, but he was not so weak as to allow Silla to change the man he was. Unwittingly, Deighton's passive aggression was more effective in upsetting Silla's plans than physical confrontation or out right rebellion. It was her constant nagging and know-it-all attitude that infuriated

Deighton the most. He often told Silla: "You's God, you must know." It was this God-like role of Silla's that finally pushed Deighton away from the family. It eventually pushed him over board into a watery grave at sea.

Despite her rock-like exterior and her intimidating persona, Silla was capable of occasional relapse into "softness." For instance, at the wedding of "Gatha's daughter, Silla missed her husband as she watched other husbands sitting by their wives. Though she tried to mask her sadness, Selina "detected a masked but unutterable longing in her glance." Even when she was seemingly happy dancing with an old man, she was jolted with passion when she suddenly saw Deighton who was recovering from the same jolt of passion on seeing his wife: "Strangely, the same passion lanced her eyes-stronger, more urgent than his even. It reached out across the hall to claim him, to confess that despite what they had both done, despite their silence, they were joined always." Silla would have loved to rush into her husband's arms, but her pride prevented her. When Deighton had the accident, Silla was genuinely sorry and regretted her desire for vengeance. Even as she had Deighton arrested, her heart was bleeding as she watched him brought so low. And she spoke the truth when she told Selina that she didn't mean to send him to his death. She did it to spare him further embarrassment and public humiliation.

Silla displayed her motherly affection the night Selina physically attacked her and called her Hitler for deporting her father: "For a long time there was only the sodden sound of struck flesh and the shouted name. Selina struck until her arms were too heavy to lift. Her rage died reluctantly . . . Clinging to the mother she slept. For a long time Silla cradled Selina in her arms as she slept. She gently and reverently caressed her tear-stained face and smoothed her tangled hair. For once, Silla displayed the emotions of a mother who recovered a missing child. With Deighton gone, she felt terribly possessive now of Selina; each caress declared that she was touching something which was finally hers alone.

One can easily compile a catalogue of negative adjectives to describe Silla. Yet, there is something tragically noble about her character. Silla understood her world and struggled to find her space in it. She expressed the normal human desire for self advancement and she played by the rules to work her way up and stay there. She understood the nature of power and she would not sugarcoat the ugliness and dirt associated with staying in power. Silla was not jealous of those better placed in life but she would struggle to pull her self up to their level.

Silla's loyalty to her family was unquestionable. She allowed her cheating husband to indulge his fancies because she grudgingly respected his manhood. But most importantly, she never undermined the healthy relationship between Deighton and their daughters-his lady-folks, whom he truly loved. She would rather live with Deighton the way he was than have him desert her and their children. Silla would share her husband with his concubines, but she could not deal with the reality of totally losing him to some bogus religious cult, a cult that emasculated him and reduced him to the status of a dependent minor. Thus, Selina was probably right when she accused her mother of deporting Deighton "because you knew he was never coming back to you."

Although Silla had more than her share of unflattering character traits but we do not hate her. We might recoil from some of her methods in pursuing her goals but we are still compelled to give credit to this resolute, no nonsense woman; a woman who was able to hold her own in a world where "you best be swift, if not somebody come and trample you quick enough."

SELINA: THE OTHER SIDE OF THE COIN

Selina the daughter and younger version of Silla, is a replica of her mother in terms of her entrenched and unassailable womanself. Silla sensed her daughter's fierce self-assurance and the close resemblance in their characters. It could be said that Selina was probably the only person that Silla was afraid of because she always acted with caution around her. Selina displayed a certain attitude of disdain towards her people, especially people like her mother who were determined to live the American dream. She felt alienated from every segment of her society whose values she despised.

Like her mother, Selina took control of her life from pre-adolescent years. She followed her own mind and did what she felt like doing, not minding what the adults or her peers felt she should do. Instead of playing outside with children her age, she preferred to lurk like a cat, behind the stairs in the dim hallway of their building. She often startled the adults who stumbled upon her in the hallway at odd hours of the day. She sometimes frightened them with the terrifying stare of her big eyes. Describing those eyes, the author said: They were not the eyes of a child. Something too old lurked in their centers. They were weighted it seemed, with scenes of a long life. She might have been old once and now, miraculously, young again-but with the memory of that other life intact. She seemed to know the world down there in the dark hall and beyond for what it was.

Selina was the complete opposite of her best friend Beryl who was too girlish and docile. Beryl had no idea of what it meant to have a self or a mind of her own. She looked forward to playing whatever role in life that her father had mapped out for her. At twelve, Beryl was already planning her married life. She told Selina: "I'm only having two children when I get married. A boy and a girl. The boy first." But such talks infuriated Selina who yelled: "I' m not having any. I' m never getting married . . . I hate boys." As for menstruation, she proudly told Beryl: "It's never gonna happen to me." Beryl persisted in getting through to her this time:

"If it doesn't happen by the time you're twenty you die."

"Well then I'll just die,"

"It'll happen. It hurts sometimes and it makes you miserable in the summer and you can't jump rope when you have it but it gives you a nice figure after a time.'

"How come?"

"I dunno. It just does. Look what's happening to Ina."

"Well if it ever happens to me nobody'll ever know. They'll see me change and think it's magic."

"Besides, it makes you feel important."

"How could anyone walking around dripping blood feel important?"

"It's funny but you do. Almost as if you were grown-up. It's like . . . oh, it's hard to explain to a kid . . ."

"Who's a kid?"

"You, because you haven't started yet."

"I'll never start!"

The whole idea of a woman being affirmed and defined by her menstrual cycle was disgusting to Selina. She felt betrayed by her mother for telling her that she was more woman than Ina. Why wasn't she told of the one important condition? Selina found it very strange that Beryl and the other girls seemed excited of their position and role of womanbeing. Worse still, Beryl was content to follow the plans that her father had laid out for her and her conversation rarely deviated from the topic of what her father wanted her to do or become. "My father wants me to be a lawyer since I am the oldest. What does your father want you to be?" she asked Selina. "He never said I had to be anything," she yelled. "Doesn't he care?" Beryl insisted. "Of course he cares."

When they all started college, Beryl entertained them with her usual prattle of her father's plans for her. Her father wanted her to study either Law or Medicine. Then she turned to Selina and asked: "What're you gonna take up Selina?" "I don't have the vaguest idea," she replied. But Beryl continued with what her father said, or thought or planned on her behalf. Selina lashed out:

"I mean what do you say about anything? You begin everything with 'My father says this or that' or 'My father's gonna give me this or that'-but what do you say, what do you want?"

"I don't understand. I say the same thing he says. Why would you ask something like that? What's wrong with what he says, or what he's gonna give me? What's your father gonna give you?" Beryl asked.

It was too late for Beryl to take the last question back. She felt terribly sorry for she had forgotten that Selina's father was dead. Selina turned away to prevent Beryl from seeing the tears that stood in her eyes. She wasn't really crying because her father was dead. She was crying because she couldn't get Beryl and the others to understand the intangible but life-sustaining gifts of love and warmth that her father had given her. Selina had always wondered how a living human being could be so devoid of the sense of self. How could a person just be a puppet on a string? Selina would rather be poor but free and in control of her destiny. Being free to choose and act on one's choices are Selina's paramount values, after all, those are the defining features of womanself.

Given her young age, Selina's strong aversion for material things was abnormal. This was even more striking because she lived in an environment where people measured human worth by material possessions and accomplishments. For instance, she disliked the "chic" clothing and fineries that girls and women made so much of. She even hated to wear curls and bows in her hair. She hated her sister for her fragile nature and lady-like ways. Looking at Ina with her faint lipstick and gloved hands, Selina thought of college girls with their graceful poses and mild manners; she couldn't identify with them. However, she knew that her mother liked to see her look and act "girlish" and she sometimes indulged her. Therefore, for the wedding of 'Gatha's daughter, Selina dressed the way her mother wanted her to, even though she felt strange and uncomfortable:

Selina stood in the parlor feeling that she did not quite belong to herself. She was owned by the yellow taffeta gown her father had bought her, her feet imprisoned in the new shoes, her fingers estranged in gloves and her wrists bound by the gold bangles she wore on such occasions. What annoyed her most was a large bow which held up her curls.

Also, on the day she was riding back home in a bus with her mother after upsetting her with her unannounced visit to her workplace, Selina tried to humor her mother by removing her hat to show her the curls that Miss Thompson had done on her hair that afternoon. The gesture worked like magic and her mother's anger gave way to a sudden softness and grudging admiration as she muttered: "I guess you think you's a full woman now with yuh few curls and can walk streets 'pon a night." Selina said she came when it was still light and turned to show her the back of her head. Silla was visibly pleased and in feigned anger said: "But look at my crosses! Curls and all now. And taking trolley this time of night by sheself. Oh God, a force-ripe woman!" Silla's rage seemed to return as she recalled the extreme effort she made to stop herself from striking Selina in front of her white colleagues at work. She looked sternly at Selina and said:

"But I got a mind to do it now. You's too own-way. You's too womanish! I tell yuh, I wun dare strike you now 'cause I'd forget my strength and kill you. But look at you. You like you living your old days first. But where you come outta, nuh? Yuh's just like my mother. A woman that did think the world put here for she. Silla correctly hit on Selina's superiority complex for she always felt she didn't belong with her people. As always, tender moments seemed to intensify the love-hate relationship between mother and daughter. Their conversation now turned to items of clothing displayed at shop windows and Silla remarked: "I see two dresses I want for you and Ina to wear to 'Gatha Steed daughter wedding. I tell you, there's one thing 'bout money. It can buy anything you see there in those store windows." Selina was offended by her mother's remark and she spoke out in anger: "Some people don't care about those things in the store windows." Silla was stung to the quick and she asked:

"But what you talking? What kind of people is they?"

"Ordinary people."

"What they does care 'bout then?"

"Other things."

"Like what?"

"I dunno. Things they don't get in stores. I dunno."

"I bet you don know. What kind of things is they, Miss Know-it-all?"

"I said I didn't know. Well, take "Gatha Steed. She could buy her daughter that pretty gown in the store window, but she can't buy any love there . . ."

"But look at my crosses! Look who talking 'bout love! What you know 'bout it? You might go hide yourself! Love! Curls! Taking trolley by sheself! I tell you, the heat from the hot comb must be sending you off. Love what!"

"Well, that's not in the stores, is it? And some people want it bad . . . Or breath, that's not in the stores either, and everybody wants that."

"Love! Give me a dollar in my hand any day! Oh, I can see what you gon give, soul. I can see from the way you think now that you ain gon amount to much. Scorning work and money like the father before you."

"I'm not scorning it. I'd just like it for one thing, so we could leave soon and go to live on Daddy's land."

For a child, Selina had an unusual disposition toward the spiritual. She was clearly on a different level when it came to what was important in life. For her mother and the Bajan community, it was all about money and its purchasing power. For Selina, money was powerless and worthless when it came to "acquiring" those invisible but life affirming values, like love, happiness or even life-giving breath. Selina drove home her point by citing the current case of 'Gatha who "bought" a husband for her daughter, yet she couldn't purchase love and happiness for the young forlorn bride. For Silla, her daughter's perspective on abstract notions like love and happiness, only confirmed her thoughts that Selina, like Deighton would not amount to much. Despite her mother's opinion of her worthless abstract values, she knew she would never follow in her mother's money-grabbing path. In fact, Selina would even "hitch a ride in a boat" back to her island without a penny in her pocket. Her own fulfillment would be settling on the island where she would roam free.

Selina's spiritual nature accounts for her inclination toward the Arts. She had the gift of poetry; she wrote and recited her poems to her classmates in elementary school. It was at that time that Beryl got the impression that Selina would be a "professional" poet while the other girls aspired to teaching, legal and medical professions. At college she enrolled in a Dance class and thrilled her classmates with her brilliant performances on the dance floor. The evening that she performed "Life Cycle" on stage, the audience was enraptured by her exquisite performance. Margaret followed her backstage and whispered to her: "Selina, I had a catharsis. I swear. All term in Greek drama I've been trying to figure out what it was and now I know. I had one. When you started dying I felt I was dying, I'm drained. Purged. Oh, you were so Greek!"

Later, her friend Rachel came to congratulate her: "You were so good, Boyce, it was frightening." Selina said she felt the same way watching Rachel dance: "It is frightening. Because you know that if you go on you'll almost fly out of yourself. That's what you want but still, in a way, it scares you." Selina was truly in her element on that night of her triumph. As a true artist, Selina always felt alienated from the material world. She always felt like flying out of herself and away from the crowd.

One can claim that it was Selina's love for the Arts that colored her vision of Clive, the poor starving artist, despised by his community! She fell truly in love with Clive because she believed he was a "real" artist. Though Clive wasn't accomplishing anything in his painting, Selina was quick to invest her meager pocket money on painting accessories for Clive. Thinking that she had found a soul-mate, she was confident that she could rekindle his interest in his work and probably help him make something of himself. Furthermore, Selina had a weakness for underdogs and Clive was a true Bajan underdog, just like Selina's father had been. She would do anything to support and protect him as she did her father. On the whole, being spiritual rendered Selina more humane toward the down trodden. It was for that reason that she struggled to protect her father from her mother's treacherous schemes. It was for the same reason that she kept company with "odd fellows" like Suggie, Miss Mary and Miss Thompson, to her mother's chagrin.

Selina was the younger version of her mother but only in a limited way. Their point of similarity included proclaiming and displaying their selfhood and independence from an early age. Both were obstinate and tenacious in following through with whatever they set their minds to accomplish even if it involved deceit or betrayal of people close to them. Silla and Selina were fearless, bold and courageous beyond compare. Selina's display of courage wasn't as dramatic as her mother's. She did not work in cane fields from sunup to sundown. She did not hawk mangoes to supplement her income. She did not scrub floors on weekdays and cook ethnic foods on weekends for extra income. And she did not operate complicated massive factory machines. Yet, Selina displayed her boldness and courage in other ways. She had the courage to be who she was despite peer pressure and her mother's desire for her to be otherwise. She had the courage to stand in front of her peers and denounce their Association, a popular project that the entire Bajan community took pride in. It took a lot of courage to confound her best friend Beryl when she asked her what role she played in the plans her father laid out for her.

However, the greatest demonstration of Selina's fearlessness and courage was the way she constantly challenged her mother. She kept her mother on tiptoe, always looking behind her shoulder for fear of being caught in her devious plans by Selina. The evening that Selina went to her mother's workplace to confront her, she was literally drunk with courage. She had planned to denounce Silla for planning to do something with Deighton's land behind his back. When she finally saw the awful-looking machines and the expert way her mother was attuned to their rhythm, she couldn't but acknowledge her mother's immense strength. In perceiving the maching-like quality of her mother's being, Selina was humbled and disarmed:

Watching her, Selina felt the familiar grudging affection seep under her amazement. Only the mother's own formidable force could match that of the machines; only the mother could remain indifferent to the brutal noise. How, then, could Selina hope to intimidate her with a few mild threats? Selina almost laughed at her own effrontery.

Nonetheless, the sight of Selina made the mother freeze: The mother turned, frowning, and as she saw Selina, her body stiffened with shock, some word of exclamation died on her lips. Silla thought that something terrible had happened at home, otherwise, what would make Selina come alone at such late hour to her mother's workplace? Yes, Selina was the second head-bull and her presence intimidated her counterpart-her mother.

When Silla finally had Deighton deported, Selina attacked her mother verbally and physically later that night. As she pounded Silla's body with her fists, she called her "Hitler"-the devil incarnate. When her father was hurt and her mother wouldn't reveal the hospital he was in, Selina was frantic. She told her mother that she was lying. She swore and threatened to call every hospital in the city to find her father. She would not accept her mother's words until she explained why her father didn't want his daughters to see him at the hospital.

The night that she sat speechless and absorbed the scalding racist insults that Margaret's mother heaped on her, Selina cursed herself for not fighting back. But in reality, Selina's sangfroid and silence were in fact, a demonstration of her defiance and noble deportment. She did not dignify her attacker's insults with counter insults.

Selina's final act of courage was her return alone, against all odds, to her native land. As she was leaving the city behind, she suddenly felt like leaving some sort of souvenir for the people:

But she had nothing. She had left the mother and the meeting hall wearing only the gown and her spring coat. Then she remembered the two silver bangles she had always worn. She pushed up her coat sleeve and stretched one until it passed over her wrist, and, without turning, hurled it high over her shoulder.

Just like her mother left her island at eighteen for a promising future in the United States, Selina is heading back to the same island, at the same age, to an uncertain future.

Another point of similarity was their fierce loyalty to family. Selina's love for her father was immeasurable. To her, Deighton was no less than a demigod and her fawning on him infuriated Silla to no end. For instance, when Silla caught Selina eavesdropping on her conversation with Florrie regarding what she would do with Deighton's land, she pushed Selina away saying: "Oh I know. I know I isn't to do a thing against your beautiful-ugly father. He's Christ to you. But wait. Wait till I finish with him. He gon be Christ crucified." Selina protected her father from her mother's schemes like a lioness her cubs.

When Deighton had the accident, Selina was angry with the machine as if it were sentient: "Couldn't the machine have seen that he was already crushed inside? Couldn't it have spared him?" She even sympathized with Deighton when he moved to live with the cult. She visited him often and helped him with his laundry sometimes. She was there washing his socks when her mother arrived with the immigration officer to arrest Deighton. It was that unforgivable act that made Selina vow revenge on her mother.

Though in constant battle with her mother, Selina still had respect and hidden affection for her. For instance, she knew that her mother hated her friendship with Clive and warned her to break it up. She told her mother that she had stopped seeing Clive. But she lied out of respect for her mother; she lied to flatter her mother's ego. Selina did not feel happy watching her mother in her various struggles with people and with life itself. She never wished her mother to fail in her plans. Therefore, when Deighton squandered the nine hundred dollars Selina was genuinely sorry for her mother. After Deighton's dramatic distribution of his purchases and Silla's smashing of the trumpet, it was Selina who stayed to comfort her mother and to gather up the wreckage of the day:

She remained. Obscurely she knew that this was her place, that for some reason she would always remain behind with the mother. For there was a part of her that always wanted the mother to win, that loved her dark strength and the tenacious lift of her body.

Just as she always protected her father, she was always nearby painfully watching her mother's moods and aggravations. She felt her mother's pain when she was the only woman sitting alone without a husband at the wedding. She could read her mother's desire for her husband in her face and Selina was truly full of pity for her mother. She was crushed when her father finally showed up and didn't hook up with her mother but was instead booed out of the reception hall.

Selina was different in several ways from her mother. Selina was a spiritual person. She was more sensitive to people's suffering than Silla, hence her penchant for the underdogs. She definitely scoffed at money for its own sake. While Silla would cry: "Give me a dollar in my hand any day," Selina would say, "Give me love all the time." While Silla issued her threats to get even with this person or that obstacle, Selina yelled her disgust and spite of her people's values. Selina's self assurance could be seen in the fact she was probably the only human who looked forward to a lonely life and an uncertain future in a foreign environment.

WOMAN CONDITION
AND EDUCATION

Formal or informal, education is a double-edged means of imparting knowledge to an individual. The most important role of education is that of an antidote to ignorance. In that capacity, education is a curative, life saving force. It has liberating and transformational powers. Therefore, an educated person is supposedly empowered with knowledge to confront issues and situations, analyze them and act judiciously.

The negative edge of education is its ability to create a mindset that is resistant to new ideas or changes. This negative edge is the one that dominates woman condition. When it is in place, no type of education can change a womanbeing into a womanself.

Self is innate but is encased within Being. It takes an individual's will power to liberate her self from her being. Very few exceptional female children start life with undamaged or unfettered selves and continue that way to the end of their lives. We have some female characters who fit the profile. We have Pilate, Silla and her daughter Selina, Efuru, Shug and

Sofia. Majority of characters either spend their lives in a state of womanbeing or break free into womanself.

Emerging from being to self is completely dependent upon human will. The claim that formal education empowers the educated to question and reject unjust rules and treatments is debatable at best. Most of the characters in this study have shown that formal education is not a prerequisite for self-reclamation. On the other hand, lack of formal education is not a pre-condition for womanbeing.

There are several characters who had informal education and yet they ended up as powerful selves. We have Pilate Dead, the ultra womanself who forced "regular" people to respect her space and her way of life. There is Efuru, who, by her example forced her community to recognize that a woman can find fulfillment in endeavors other than childbearing. Though Efuru respected the traditions of her people, she bent them to her will and still gained the respect and admiration of her people. Silla Boyce did not go to school yet her womanself was unassailable. She became a role model for her peers and a pillar of strength for the Bajan community in New York. Silla's daughter Selina demonstrated her womanself in more subtle ways. Though young, she took on the Bajan community in a kind of battle of values. She was the griot of her people and she was the one who returned to the island homeland to reconnect with the authentic values of her people. Shug Avery, the free spirited cabaret singer swooped into town and rescued Celie from the stranglehold of her enslaving husband. Though Celie's metamorphosis remained unfinished, it was thanks to Shug that she evolved as far as she did. Sofia was too sure of herself to take an insult from a white mayor's wife. She was so secure in herself that she did not think twice when she returned a blow to the mayor. It took the law to subdue Sofia. Her self seemed to have retreated while she was incarcerated but it was much alive to intimidate the mayor's wife when Sophia ended up working for her.

Several educated characters were pushed into womanbeing despite their education. The sixteen-year old Janie had some education. She started life as a promising womanself. Janie wanted to live out her fantasy about love and marriage by running away from an ill-matched marriage to an old man. She ended up in another marriage that stripped her of her self for twenty years. It was Joe's death that freed Janie and set her on course to self-recovery.

Ruth Foster, the wealthy daughter of the first black doctor in town, had some education. Yet, her education and upper class status did not save her from the worst case of womanbeing in her marriage to Macon Dead. Both Ruth and Janie were moderately educated compared to Ruth's daughters Magdalene and First Corinthians. Magdalene with her high school education and Corinthians with her college education and polished French manners remained "unused" and trapped in womanbeing in their father's house.

We find the school teacher, Amaka groveling on her knees before her mother-in-law, begging her not to throw her out because of her presumed barrenness. Amaka bought into her culture that made motherhood the only condition for self-fulfillment. It would take the shocking act of near-homicide to wrench her out of her married home after six years of verbal and physical abuses. It was her uneducated mother, not her education that convinced her that the words, husband and man mean different things. It was her will power that finally released her self from her being.

In Bessie Head's *Maru*, we find Margaret and Dikeledi. Magaret is a school-teacher and Dikeledi obtained a certificate in childhood education from England. Yet, neither of them had any self to be reckoned with. Margaret is saddled with her memory of an orphan raised as a scientific experiment by her foster mother Margaret senior. She could care less about humane treatment. Besides, the inferiority of her Masarwa origin got her disposed to expecting and accepting all kinds of abuses from people. Her friend Dikeledi had her privileged life of a princess. She had her comfortable house and her car. Yet, she flaunted her sexuality to get the attention of the ugly Moleka, her inferior in many respects. Both Margaret and Dikeledi considered themselves lucky to be among the countless women in town who served as sex toys to Moleka and the paramount chief Maru. Dikeledi was only too happy to marry Moleka after she succeeded in getting pregnant by him. Margaret, the prized trophy that both men fought over, was literally hauled away by Maru whom she did not love. She had no say in being whisked away by one man while her heart was set on another: "What could she say, except that at that moment she would have chosen anything as an alternative to the living death into which she had so unexpectedly fallen?" Margaret must learn to love Maru as her husband and Moleka had to settle with Dikeledi, the next best woman on earth.

Fusena in Aidoo's *Changes* is also a trained teacher. She married her classmate Ali. That marriage stripped her of her self, took away her profession and turned her into a kiosk keeper. Like her other African sisters, she was powerless before her culture and religion, thus, she settled into her role as a mute first wife of Ali. Her only discomfort was having a university graduate as co-wife.

Esi, Fusena's co-wife fared even worse. She walked off her first marriage charging her husband of marital rape, a concept that scandalized and angered her mother and grandmother. To these elder women, a husband could never rape his wife. He had the right to sex with his wife any time he wanted. Therefore, Esi was being foolish with her "civilized" ideas. Esi with her well paying job and her house, not to talk of her college degree, was hardly out of her first marriage when she fell victim to another marriage! This time, she found herself in the humiliating position of a second wife. With her status and liberated view of sex in marriage, one expected Esi to be wiser in her next encounter with potential husbands. But Esi lost her self in what the author describes as love, love of a man who used her to demonstrate his culture cum religious privilege to multiple wives. Perhaps, Aidoo is right in subtitling her novel, *A Love Story*. Because there is no other way to rationalize Esi's decision to give up all she had gained only to become first, a concubine, then a second wife. Temporarily she felt that marrying Ali fulfilled her dreams of independence. Ali was not on her back every one of every twenty-four hours of every day. In fact, he was hardly ever near her at all. In that sense she was extremely free and extremely contented.

Esi woke up to her stupidity in no time. Less than a year after their marriage Ali developed love interest in his secretary; he started giving her rides home after work. Esi saw Ali less and less. Even on national holidays like Christmas and New Year Ali didn't show up at her house. Very soon she couldn't cope any more; she had to rely on tranquilizers. She realized the marriage was a dead end; she was fed up with Ali coming when and if he felt like seeing her. Finally she confronted Ali:

"Ali, I can't go on like this."

"Like what?"

"Like this. This is no marriage"

"What would you consider to be a marriage?"

"I don't know. But if this is it, then I'm not having any of it."

"If that's how you see it, then I'm going."

"Well, just go 'home' to your wife and children and leave me alone."

Esi broke up with Ali though she never bothered to have the marriage annulled. They became just good friends "who found it convenience once in a while to fall into bed and make love", says the author. Perhaps, that's what it should have been for a truly self secure woman who knew what she wanted in a relationship. Esi felt very miserable and she literally broke down and wept at her misadventure with Ali.

Maiguru in *Nervous Conditions* had a Master's degree in Philosophy. She had a good job, a good husband and two children. She had a house servant and she was driven wherever she wanted to go by her husband. Yet, her education and worldly possessions could not save her from the misery of womanbeing. Maiguru was silenced throughout her marriage. She was just an obedient housewife with no access to the salary she earned. Her opinion was not sought in any decisions her husband made for their family. She was so cooped up in her marriage that her daughter vicariously felt her entrapment. She was so intimidated by her husband that she could not protect her daughter from his verbal and physical abuses. The informal education she received from her culture made her value marital "security" more than self-autonomy.

Ramatoulaye and Aissatou are perhaps the only women who drew from their formal education to combat a threatening state of womanbeing. Ramatoulaye stood her ground and staked her claim to raise her children in the home she had built with her erring husband. She would not be cowered into seclusion while the offending husband went about cavorting with his teenage second wife. Because of her education, Ramatoulaye was able to look the situation in the eye and face up to it and prevail.

Aissatou on her part, brought to bear her westernized perception of love. She refused to share her beloved husband with another woman. For her husband to even think of mating with a woman he did not love was despicable to Aissatou. Aissatou knew she could start life over on her own. She went in for more education in order to support herself and her four sons. She was so self assured that she "committed" the unprecedented act of taking her children out of the country to raise on her own.

For Ramatoulaye and Aissatou, it was not just their education that freed them; it was also their will to assert their rights as selves. They refused to be beaten down and they would not allow their selves to retreat into mere beings. For the greater number of women, education without will power was not enough to ensure selfhood. For those who had the will, neither formal nor informal education stood in their way to self assertion and self actualization.

BIBLIOGRAPHY

NOVELS

Aidoo, Ama Ata. *Changes: A Love Story*, London: The Women's Press Ltd. 1991

Ba, Mariama. *So Long a Letter*, London: Heinemann, 1980

Dangarembga, Tsitsi. *Nervous Conditions*, Harare: Zimbabwe Publishing House, 1988

Emecheta, Buch, *The Joys of Motherhood*, London: Heinemann, 1979

Head, Bessie. *Maru*, Heinemann-African Writers Series, 1972

Hurston, Zora Neal. *Their Eyes Were Watching God*, New York: Harper & Row Publishers, 1990

Marshall Paule. *Brown Girl, Brownstones*, New York: The Feminist Press, 1981

195

Morrison, Toni. *Song of Solomon*, New York: Signet, New American Library, 1978

Nwapa, Flora. *Efuru*, London: Heinemann, 1966

_____. *One Is Enough*, Enugu, Tana Press Ltd. 1981.

Walker, Alice. *The Color Purple*, New York: Simon & Schuster (Pocket Books), 1982.

OTHER WORKS CITED

Borchert, Donald M. Editor-in-chief, "Being Process," in *The Encyclopedia of Philosophy Supplement*, New York: Simon &Schuster, 1996.

Craig, Edward. General Editor, *Routledge Encyclopedia of Philosophy*, Vol.1, pages 699-701.

_____, *Routledge Encyclopedia of Philosophy*, Vol. 4, pages 521-524.

_____, *Routledge Encyclopedia of Philosophy*, Vol.8, pages-632-637.

Edwards, Paul. Editor-in-chief, The *Encyclopedia of Philosophy*, Vol.1, pages 273-276

_____, The *Encyclopedia of Philosophy*, Vol. 5, pages 95-97.

Magill, Frank N. Editor, *World Philosophy*: Essay-Reviews of 225 Major works, 1932-1971, pages 2082-2085 and pages 2271-2272.

McLeish, Kenneth. *Key Ideas in Human Thought*, London: Book Creation Services, 1993, pages 668-669.

Roeckelein, Jon E. *Dictionary of Theories, Laws & Concepts in Psychology*, Westport: Greenwood Press, 1998, pages 353-354.